Turbulent Seas

My Life in the American Merchant Marine

*(Retired Captain) Lance Orton
and Barnett Singer*

PERSONAL CHRONICLE 1
BENNINGTON, VERMONT
2012

First Edition published in 2010 by the Merriam Press

Second Edition (2012)

Copyright © 2010 by Lance Orton and Barnett Singer
Book design by Ray Merriam
Additional material copyright of named contributors.

ISBN 978-1475265538
Merriam Press #PC1-P

This work was designed, produced, and published in
the United States of America by the

Merriam Press
133 Elm Street Suite 3R
Bennington VT 05201

E-mail: ray@merriam-press.com
Web site: merriam-press.com

The Merriam Press is always interested in publishing new manuscripts on military history, as well as reprinting previous works, such as reports, documents, manuals, articles and other material on military history topics.

Contents

Introduction

THE adventure side of this future merchant mariner's life, including as a tanker captain, was prompted, I believe, by my parents each summer of my youth (from the time I was about five) dedicating vacations to exploring some part of the U.S. with their children. And of all the driving expeditions we took from Buffalo, New York, the trip to Alaska was the *pièce de résistance*, the summit! I think that was the one which had the greatest influence on my future choice of career. Naturally my parents worked hard all year to make these vacations possible. We would end up driving many hundreds of miles to see different locales, and I don't recall any of my playmates in elementary or even high school days having such experiences. From circa 1952, we would be out in the elements those summers, and often camping in tents, where there was sometimes the risk of animals attacking, of poisonous snake bites, and the like. We went up and down the East coast to see the ocean and its beaches, and to other parts of the U.S.; but it seemed like each trip sparked more interest for the next one. As a boy, I especially wanted to know what lay beyond the next mountain, lake, or pass. My parents and simply the astonishing, varied environments we beheld made all this very exciting for a boy, and I'm certain that such experiences, especially the Alaska trip, kindled my desire to travel and explore, and as it turned out, to suffer and grow abroad as an adult.

But why a new account here of life in the American Merchant Marine? First, because there are few books on the subject, and this one is a real departure from works like John McPhee's *Looking for a Ship* (1990), or John Butler's more general history of the U.S. Merchant Marine (*Sailing on Friday*, 1997). Second, because no existence is the same as any other, and ours has become the age of the memoir, and one, too, where the military (broadly put) remains at the forefront of American concerns. In my case, I really believe I experienced an interesting, hectic, and often dangerous life on the high seas, and in a variety of ports from the mid-'60s through to the mid-1980s. What to me were fascinatingly difficult human challenges began with my cadet days and from my earliest times on the water, then continued during my first voyages as a third officer, and through my appointment as one of the youngest American captains of a very large vessel—in fact, the largest American ship ever built at that time (late '70s): *The Golden Endeavor*, then classed as a supertanker, but later downgraded to "Baby Super."

There have been numerous written accounts of the natural hazards Mother Nature flings at mariners—from the craze a few years back for icebergs (owing in part to the movie *Titanic*), to storms of various intensities, including hurricanes, typhoons, and tidal waves et al. In my career I encountered all of those, but to some degree, an experienced mariner can predict these natural phenomena, especially in a technologically advanced era. Far less predictable—and the real subject of this book—is the human behavior I encountered aboard ships during long constrained voyages and also, in ports, including in the pre-Gorbachev Soviet Union, dominated by the KGB and full of corruption.

In the age of sail men were confined to maybe 100 or 120 feet of ship, where today we might have 1200 feet of steel at our disposal. But I don't think the psychology of humans in a maritime environment has changed that greatly. People inherently dislike limits, and prolonged constraints help alter behaviors, sometimes disastrously so. The potential hazards that men pose to other men (and women) have not really changed a lot over the years. Envy, greed, rage, prevarication—those human infirmities and predilections still abound, and I saw and confronted them all, sometimes with heart pounding. But I also saw goodness, and I saw it die.

Ascending the ladder of the Merchant Marine, I sailed with colorful, crazy, but sometimes gifted maritime personnel, and fought off a number of life-threatening situations, including pirate attacks, knife fights on board ship, attempted poisonings (of me), etc. I also sailed to Vietnam in the years when a merchant mariner literally took his life in his hands doing so. I had to deal with accidents and near explosions on ships, due to volatile hydrocarbons and other material we carried, but also to human error. I had to work with recalcitrant, potentially violent longshoremen; drunken crew members carrying a lot of inner anger and incompetence on ship and off; and careerists or sadists who didn't mind inflicting their unfairness on subalterns. But as noted, I also got to work with the noble and the utterly reliable. If this book seems a bit skewed in the direction of idiosyncratic, scheming, or downright maniacal characters in action, maybe that's because those are the stories that still stand out in my mind, and which I thought would interest today's readers.

I endured a lot of situations that *were* downright dramatic, at least to me; and I learned a lot and matured a good deal on the high seas, as well as in ports where we docked. Along the way I divested myself of numerous illusions. I'm a baby boomer, but I don't think my experience was typical for most of that generation. However, many lined up, then crowded video/DVD stores for films like *Titanic*; many seem to have a taste for adventure, if only vicarious, and many seem to love anything related to the water. As they gain more and more leisure time, baby boomers and others might be curious to know what life on the high seas *really* involves, and has involved, from a human perspective.

In this book they get the inside story. They also get a close view of American organizations both blessed and plagued by a variety of personalities, and especially, by the growing disease of bureaucratization and political maneuvering. And they encounter a sad, yet comical Soviet Union before Gorbachev, where the secret police, inequities, and paranoia were rife. Not to sound overly moralistic, readers should see here how evil must always be fought with good. It always was that way, and despite societal attempts to be "different" the past several decades, it always will be.

Since retiring from the Merchant Marine, I've settled down to a busy and full life of being an independent air and water purification expert/installer—owning my own corporation, working for clients like the American Cancer Society, blessed with an enriching family life in the Greater Buffalo area, and often heard on the subject of health, and water or air quality on radio or in lectures. But that more violent, dog-eat-dog past of life in the Merchant Marine—stretching from the '60s to the '80s—still lies within me, and it is a story that I hope will compel readers' attention. So—onward with one man's turbulent life on the high seas. Let's start off with a bang from my early years on the water—literally and figuratively!

Chapter 1

My Baptism at Sea
with Captain Crofton

THE high suicide rate of Merchant Marine captains might shock people without experience in the maritime industry, and certainly it would have shocked me when I was starting out in the métier. I would come to realize, however, that captains, like other crew members, could be a quirky, eccentric breed, and my second voyage to sea under Captain Sam Crofton[1] is a case in point. This voyage began December 5, 1969—on the *S.S. Constitution State*. I had just been married on November 14 of that year to Susan Knoll—from a family in Buffalo. Joining my ship in harbor at the Brooklyn Piers, I was no stranger to New York City, having attended college in that area. The ship was being loaded with various cargoes for a long voyage—revolvers, ammo, alcohol, military equipment (including tanks and jeeps), personal vehicles for military personnel in the Philippines, Japan, etc. There was plenty of handshake cargo, i.e. two hands on the sides of bags of grain or flour. Stencilled on the side of these bags was a logo denoting charitable—mainly Catholic—organizations to disburse this material to foreign governments for them in turn to distribute, or in many cases, to rip off.

Our voyage was to start in New York Harbor, then wind down the Jersey Shore to Philadelphia along the East Coast through the C and D Canal to Baltimore, continuing down the Atlantic Coast—Norfolk to Savannah to the Florida Straits. In each port we'd pick up more and more "break bulk cargo," as we called it. The ship was of World War II vintage (a C-3), and this was long before container ships became standard. Instead, there were old sticks, booms, and guy wires on this five-hatch vessel.

The whole trip would be new and different for me (given that my first voyage had been on a tanker from the East Coast to India and back, rounding the Cape of Good Hope). I had never been on a break bulk ship before. As the vessel's third officer and only twenty-two, I

---

[1]   This is a pseudonym.

was definitely inexperienced, and fear of the unknown seemed to be an ever-present companion. I wasn't yet sure of my cargo-handling expertise, though I *was* confident of my ability to navigate.

My initial problem was that I had never before had to deal with a group called longshoremen! They were well known by others— particularly in ports of the Northeast—for using constantly vulgar language, in fact, more vulgarity than content. They were also known for being ornery and ruthless, and in many cases, as out and out thieves.

Just after joining the ship in New York, and after only a few hours in port, I was put into a hold with these characters to discuss safe loading of cargo, proper stowage, anti-breakage policies, and the like. Little did I realize that damage and theft simply went with the territory, and that these cargo holds were dangerous to anyone who tried to be too principled on such matters. From main deck, a short thirty-six inch steel wall rose on the outer edges of the hatch opening. Coming up vertically during a loading operation, you had to be vigilant, or you could easily fall over it, then fifty or sixty feet down to the bottom of the cement hatch floor. Had such things really happened in *On the Waterfront* fashion? They had indeed—many times: to ship's crew, officers, and to longshoremen themselves. Sometimes these could be sheer accidents, or sometimes they stemmed from what was euphemistically called "outside motivation."

So here I was, within an hour or two of joining the ship, green as a proverbial dollar bill, given the task of monitoring loading by this surly contingent in the upper tween deck area. Climbing down into the wings of that deck, I beheld about twenty longshoremen, theoretically on the job. Of that number maybe one at best was actually working, while the other eighteen or nineteen were just jawing away, sleeping, or busy swilling from "accidentally" broken cases of whisky lying about. Most wore huge trench coats with literally deep pockets, in which—believe it or not—you could carry a case or more of liquor on each side.

"Where's the hatch boss?" I finally asked. Apparently hard of hearing, these layabouts simply ignored my question, continuing to play cards, drink, or whatever else they were doing. I walked into a special security locker previously loaded half full with boxed Smith and Wesson revolvers and being "finished up" with cases of alcohol, a normal way to load. In this case it was Jack Daniels whisky. Once I got inside that locker with fifteen to twenty-foot stacks of Jack Daniels, and three or four guys sitting in the corner, I again managed to eke out the same question: "Is the hatch boss around?"

One guy finally bothered to answer: "Whose askin'?" With the pride of an inexperienced seaman, I replied: "Ship's third officer." I was trying my best to impress them, but all I heard was thin laughter that echoed round the hatch, and a chorus of "oohs"—as if to say, "Big bloody deal...." Things didn't seem to be going well, and I began wondering about normal procedures here.

Finally, after rousing himself from several hours of napping, and reeking of alcohol, the hatch boss slunk out from behind a box, rubbed his eyes, and said: "Whaddya want, kid?" And I replied, still full of a neophyte officer's pride: "I want to discuss stowage of cargo, sir." With the ladder teetering, the grizzled boss followed me out of the security locker to the upper tween deck. I asked him why everybody was just sitting around here, doing no apparent work, but the man didn't bother to answer—it was obvious he was dealing with a young pup. Most of these longshoremen, I should add, were men in their forties or fifties, well seasoned in knowing how to do pretty well what they wanted to do on a job.

Anyway, the boss, having ignored my query, walked me instead to a corner of the open hatch from which, as noted, a person might easily fall all the way to the bottom of the hold, splattering his brains on the cement floor. This chief stevedore got near the edge, then called me over: "C'm here, Third Officer," he said. "I got something to show you. Before I answer your questions about how we work," he said, "I want you should take a good look to see how far it is to the bottom. OK?" I stepped over, right next to him, watching him point below. Now then, if I needed to discuss anything about the ship's loading operations, he said, I should do so with my chief officer, and *never* with longshoremen. He then topped off his brief speech with a direct invitation for me to get the hell out of there!

Sizing up the situation, and realizing my unpopularity, I thought it good advice to follow. I could easily visualize being hauled up in our chicken-wire stokeslitter as a mangled, dead corpse, so I felt it best to exit fast. I also thought I should talk the situation over with our ship's chief officer.

The chief mate was a man in his early sixties, a thin, wiry individual with a grandfatherly look, though not necessarily a kindly one, but certainly a look of experience. From many years at sea his face was weathered, as was his personality. Arriving at his office, I explained the problem I'd just encountered and saw him smile, really a half smile creeping at the corners of his mouth. He knew he was dealing with a kid. Most of these ships' officers were on the oldish side, generally in their fifties or sixties, and often World War II vets. They had learned long ago to ignore these problems posed by longshoremen, and my sole responsibility, said the chief, was to watch these loaders, but not to get within arm's length of them. I was simply to make notes about the cargo itself, damages occurring, and so on. One *never* discussed such matters with longshoremen, only with one's superiors at the end of each day. Any damages or labor activities considered unusual should be noted in the ship's log. Formal discussions about labor or a lack thereof involved *only* the chief officer or the captain, who then spoke directly to the boss of the cargo-loading operation.

Having survived my first day on board, I came to realize in hindsight that I'd been pretty lucky. In many cases those hardened buzzards wouldn't have wasted an instant pushing a callow youngster down the hatch. I also came to learn that different ports had different kinds of longshoremen. In some, stevedores were more amicable, and less given to drink, and you could reason with them a bit, first smoking a kind of peace pipe and making a treaty. In other words you might offer them a cup of coffee or something else that wasn't readily available—a sandwich from your galley, or other things normally off limits to longshoremen. New York and L.A. were downright bad, but some ports were much better. Loaders in Northern California, Oregon, and Washington often turned out to be decent, accessible human beings, and you could actually broach some of your problems to them, and they'd try to accommodate you. But in the big cities along the Northeast coast it was unheard of even to *try* discussing efficiency or proper stowage. Not only were cases of alcohol broken into on a regular basis, but so also were strong boxes of revolvers. Longshoremen would simply help themselves for use against who knew?... Or to sell them on the black market, or to the underworld? I was once told that pretty well every longshoreman on the ship had a revolver, and that I'd better keep this in mind when dealing with them.

Baptism under fire? Yes, I grew up in a hurry, and by the time the ship had finished its East Coast loading process, I knew the rules of the game. From Savannah we sailed down through the Florida Straits, and from there took the Mona Pass, separating the easternmost tip of Cuba from the western parts of Hispanola, i.e. Haiti. Then we struck a course southwestward toward the port of Cristobal, Panama, the Caribbean gateway to the Pacific. Transiting the Panama Canal, we proceeded along the west coast of Central America, and up along the Mexican coast, where we encountered huge sea turtles. Our captain loved turtle meat and deciding to slow the ship, lowered away a lifeboat, took his revolver in hand, and managed to kill a couple of the creatures. The chief cook then butchered and prepared them for the captain's dinner.

Our voyage then continued uninterrupted to Coos Bay, Oregon, where we loaded lumber, before taking on more cargo in Seattle and Port Angeles. The vessel, full of lumber stowed twenty feet high on deck across the now closed-up hatches, was by this time so jam-packed that we actually had to walk from bow to stern on huge slabs of bundled timbers. In between them we also wedged the military's tanks, secured by thirty-two massive chains and man-sized turn buckles. This concluded the loading portion of the voyage.

The captain who had been on board prior to us leaving the States now departed on vacation, relieved by a younger captain, Sam Crofton, one of the strangest I would ever encounter. My first impression was of a massive man of football lineman's proportions—a good 6'6", and over 300 pounds. Captain Crofton was naturally soft in the middle, with a ruddy doughboy's mien, and hair flying out in every direction. (I doubt he owned a comb.) When he talked, his mobile lips flopped, and you could see the saliva gathering inside. During the course of our conversations I always feared he'd shower me with spittle. However, he didn't speak all that often, and I was intrigued that he was so much younger than the chief officer or second officer. By this point I knew that the second officer had a serious drinking problem, and I was starting to have concerns about how reliable *any* advice coming from an older superior might be here. My preconceptions about humans on board were beginning to be seriously revised.

To my surprise the new skipper was only forty-eight, and this put me somewhat at ease. I thought there might be some hope that with him being younger, I would not be considered quite so green. I hoped I might even get a sympathetic ear to talk out some serious matters. But in fact, most anything I'd want to discuss had probably been hashed over many times and years before during these superiors' earlier sailing days. So my conversational desires were quite extraneous to their daily interests. In fact I kept noticing during long night watches how the older men remained unusually quiet. Lacking a love life, wives, and kids, due to a slew of divorces back home, the most important things in life had been basically stripped from their souls, leaving what I increasingly perceived as human shells on board.

This was the character of the group that now sailed from the Straits of Juan de Fuca, striking a great circle course for Yokohama, Japan. Navigation in those days still resembled navigation of previous centuries, and use of the hand instrument, the sextant, remained crucial and essential. So did knowledge of spherical trigonometry, equally important in determining courses.

My first insights into Captain Crofton's abilities, however, quickly dashed any hopes I had that he possessed good working knowledge of such matters. At one point I overheard a conversation between him and the second officer, discussing various courses to take on this "Great Circle Voyage;" and it became apparent that he was by no means a navigator. Even with his obvious drinking problems, the second officer far outshone in expertise the "old man," as we all called the skipper.

It was normal for a ship's second officer and captain to handle long-term navigational planning for a vessel, particularly celestial navigation; whereas the third officer (me) was more responsible for fixing the ship's daily position on his eight-hour watch, making sure we were steering courses that the captain had specified. If at times it was necessary to alter a course slightly, due to the potential of collision with other traffic, one didn't need to confer; but if the ship's position seemed too far from the intended track, major corrections required the captain's validation, unless there was an immediate problem for the vessel (such as reef shoals or other such dangers). At all times my duty was to maintain the ship afloat in safe waters; but whenever the captain walked out on the bridge, he automatically assumed command (or the "conn," as we called it), and orders to helm or engines always emanated from him.

Our voyage at first (and in an illusory way) proceeded uneventfully; but this was my first time traversing the Pacific, and it was an awesome experience. Seeing no *terra firma* all the way to Japan, I didn't feel bored at all. It was too exciting listening to older mens' conversations in the mess room, hearing the different things they'd endured during World War II. With some unlicensed crewmen assigned to my watch, I also had lengthy discussions of events like being torpedoed and surviving, while other friends were being killed around you. It made for a rather quick transit, because it seemed like every day there was a new adventure to entertain the mind (I didn't realize that my own lay in wait around the corner). Sponging up all this lore, I also studied the people near me, learning a lot about different personalities. I was definitely the youngest on board, the closest to me being a man in his mid-thirties; yet it felt like I was rapidly maturing beyond my years. I didn't generally interface with most unlicensed crew members, except the few assigned to my watch. However, from those I talked to,

I absorbed some of the scuttlebutt, as they called it, of what was going on, and who liked who among crew members—useful information to have.

In Japan we entered Yokohama harbor, where in the distance you could see Mount Fuji, reminding me of Rainier and other mountains of America's Pacific Northwest. It was inspirational when the weather was clear. But I had not yet spent any time in an Oriental environment, and the culture there was very different from any I had previously encountered. On this trip we only stayed ashore for brief periods—maybe four or five hours a day, scouting out souvenirs. I bought my new bride and my sister-in-law pearl necklaces, which to me were costly items, though we negotiated on all prices. Japanese people generally seemed kind, but as few then spoke English, there was a major communication barrier.

After leaving on a night departure from the shelter of Yokohama Bay and proceeding southward around the peninsula to the open Pacific, the weather on that unruly expanse of water began to change drastically, and wind and sea started lashing the ship. This was my first experience in a real Pacific storm, and now the ship began rolling from side to side and pitching up and down in a way I didn't believe possible. Frankly, it unnerved me, because I'd never seen a vessel lurch and heave like this. I also began to sense that confronted with turbulent weather the ship's captain had deep fears of his own. At least our radar had worked intermittently across the Pacific, but now, several hours out of port, it failed totally, and we were on our own, heading toward another Japanese city, Kobe.

At midnight my watch period concluded, and I went below to try and soothe my nervous stomach, wondering whether I'd have full-blown seasickness, which hadn't occurred since my first cadet voyage. That bout of vomiting had been a horrendous experience, so bad I'd wanted to kill myself, and this latest round of nausea brought back those suicidal memories. However, while in my bunk that night, the weather mercifully abated, and it was calmer out when I was called back up in the morning at seven a.m. for bridge duty.

We now proceeded to Kobe under better conditions, the crew working daily to jettison dunnage—wood used to shore up cargo in the holds, much of it expendable. The idea was to retain only the better pieces of lumber, sometimes selling or bartering them with local traders. For some U.S. sailors in these Third World countries that included bartering for a woman.

Leaving Kobe, we proceeded through an inland sea, a backdoor way of negotiating the rear of Japan, and thence to Korea. We transited that inland sea to the ports of Inchon and Pusan, well known in the Korean War, and treacherous in passage, due to high tides and heavy currents, similar to ones found along North American coasts from Maine to Nova Scotia. Again, my young mind began to realize that the skipper lacked confidence in his own abilities. Approaching Inchon, Captain Crofton summoned all officers to the bridge, each assigned a special navigational duty to call out bearings and object ranges. This was probably prudent, given our lack of radar, but I felt that my own navigational training should have sufficed. The captain seemed truly scared, displaying a highly visible nervous condition that no one else manifested. Why did he require such a large team? I wondered. After all, we were making a daylight approach on a clear day, and radar wasn't really crucial to safe passage here. We also picked up a Korean "pilot"—whenever you entered foreign waters, you almost always picked up a pilot (a local expert in the area's navigation), and he could issue orders to the ship's helm or steer the vessel, subject to the captain's approval.

But even with this pilot on board Crofton remained agitated, partly due to his inability to communicate with a newcomer who had limited English. However, we reached port safely, and for the first time in my life, I met Koreans and also tasted their cuisine, which shocked me. Their mainstay dish was *kimchee*, basically food stored in a process allowing it to rot, and concocted from any number of vegetables or other items. The taste and odor, however, were more than I could bear, and I would never try such fare again. In Korea I soon learned that I was always safe bringing a brown bag lunch ashore. Never did I become the gourmet I should perhaps have tried to become, and certainly no Korean gourmet. The only food I found palatable there was white rice, washed down with Coca-Cola, or what limited supply I could find.

From Korea we sailed southward to make landfall on the east coast of the Philippines, passing through the San Bernardino Straits into the Sulu Sea, the inland ocean separating eastern Philippine islands from western ones. This body of water connecting the South China Sea to the Pacific is shallow and treacherous, and sextant use was a constant challenge there. Making landfall on islands, and not being able to determine distances with radar, you had to be *very* adept with this instrument, used not only for celestial bodies, but to figure out distances of objects like mountains. Vertical sextant angles measured the angle of the height of the mountain to the horizon, permitting a determination of distance from islands. Via the use of trigonometry, the horizontal angles obtained also helped verify distances between islands—in fact, mathematics, so often considered useless after high school, was an essential part of safe navigation here.

Captain Crofton continued to exhibit undue fear for a man who should have had plentiful experience. During the passage through the San Bernardino Straits and into the Sulu, he kept summoning all deck officers out onto the bridge. After we made it through those straits and into a wider sea, weather conditions deteriorated, with heavy fog and rain creating extreme navigation difficulties, since water was still shallow here and currents dangerous. Radar would now have been a boon, but it was still out of commission. I should add that when I entered the maritime industry in the late '60s, radar use as a collision avoidance device was just beginning to come into its own, and in my first two or three years it often remained dysfunctional. The old sextant and navigational lead lines employed by seamen for hundreds of years were crucial.

Managing to enter the eastern part of the Sulu Sea in conditions of limited visibility, Crofton ordered the ship's engines to reduce speed. For three days we traveled westward on varying courses, using "dead reckoning," meaning we guessed at positions based on prevalent information that might or might not prove correct. All you could do was try to figure out things that typically occurred in certain currents or areas, studying all this while on watch, then making calculated guesses. Sometimes these guesses ended up on the money, but sometimes they didn't, and there was always the possibility of a truly lethal navigational decision. Crofton's high anxiety didn't help, because when a ship's captain openly reveals his jangled nerves, it obviously undermines the confidence officers should have both in him and in their own work. The mood becomes infectious.

As we approached the western exit of the Sulu Sea, there was supposed to be an island rising from the ocean's floor called Palawan Island, and a deep water passage round the southeastern portion of it, Palawan Pass, where the Sulu dumps itself into the South China Sea. Navigational problems here include numerous submerged reefs and sandbar shallows. Lacking radar, and with limited visibility, we somehow had to negotiate our passage around an island lying almost in a north-south direction. The danger was hitting the beach before getting a good sighting of that island, permitting us to change course in time.

On the afternoon of the third day, the sun began to be seen inter-mittently in the sky. I used the sextant to try and take a position in the morning hours, while the frantic captain, running to and fro from one side of the bridge to the other, also attempted to determine our posi-tion. This constant bustling about continued to make me nervous, and Crofton kept asking every few seconds, it seemed: "Did you get an ob-servation? Did you get an observation?" I did indeed manage to obtain a sunline observation, now recommending that he alter the ship's course as soon as possible! The sunline coupled with a continuing read-ing of water depth permitted me to conclude that we needed to change direction ASAP in order to avoid an impending reef, which would tear out the bottom of the ship!

Crofton's response was to impede the ship's forward movement, putting its engines on stop, which did nothing significant to lessen the danger of the vessel's forward motion carrying us onto the reef. Coast-ing with momentum, and even with our engines on stop, we continued making dangerous headway. Again, I requested in a dignified manner that we alter course from west to southwest, which I felt would safely take us down through the deepwater Palawan Pass. The captain called the chief officer to the bridge, they reviewed my sextant data, and the chief agreed with my request, forcefully suggesting that with all expe-diency Captain Crofton accept this young third officer's recommenda-tion. Which he did. Within an hour or two we could see Palawan Is-land on our starboard bow. Also the chief officer recommended to the captain that he now increase the ship's speed again, so that it could safely negotiate the passage. By late afternoon we had cleared Palawan Pass and were thankfully out into the South China Sea.

This was probably the first time I conclusively felt that I had command capability. But I also began to realize that I was dealing with some pretty odd characters, which would be borne out time and again in the next decade, encompassing my rise to Merchant Marine captain.

On entering the South China Sea we struck a course for the Straits of Singapore, allowing passage through the Molucca Straits and into the East Indian Ocean—i.e., the Bay of Bengal. During the several-day passage across the South China Sea, I felt more and more uncomfort-able about Sam Crofton's command capability; however, I kept those hesitancies to myself, never discussing them with anyone else on board. That would have been tantamount to insurrection, and it could get one brought up on charges.

We entered the Straits of Singapore on a clear morning passage, for which I was grateful. Maritime traffic in the area was traveling across the Straits to and from Singapore to Indonesia, and in both directions it was heavy. So there was still real danger—of collision with these vessels, complicated by the demands of narrow channels winding through numerous islands.

About eight-thirty in the morning, a half hour into my watch, I was surprised to see Crofton with no other officers on the bridge to help in navigation, as in the past. Apparently he had finally concluded that the ship was in safe hands with his young third officer, an exhilarating feeling for me. I guess I seemed composed and cool taking navigational bearings, and ordering course changes to the helm. But soon after he appeared on the bridge, I noticed some long boats similar to dugout canoes, constructed from large, burned-out logs and with small gas engines in the rear, moving at a speed exceeding that of our slow-moving vessel. I noticed these boats were coming in our direction off one of the islands, and that they apparently wanted to travel close under the stern of our ship. I was perplexed as to why they would come that close, and suddenly realized that there were six of them, each loaded with about seven or eight men holding long poles. It became rapidly apparent that they planned to board our ship while we were underway!

Since the captain was no longer on the bridge, I telephoned his cabin, informing him that we had boarders coming on both quarters of the ship, port and starboard—and in fact, these uninvited guests were now starting to climb up those long bamboo poles with hooks linked to the ends of them and fastened to our rails. An agitated Crofton told me to call the chief officer, notifying him of the boarding, which I did immediately, before running back out to the bridge. The minute I got there I saw that most of the boats below were emptied. The captain had now run up to the bridge, too, with a revolver in hand, which he began waving wildly. We had fallen prey to a daytime invasion of pirates, and the ship's stern was soon covered with these Oriental men of small stature, rapidly moving forward toward midship, the crew's living quarters.

While the anguished captain on the bridge continued waving his revolver like a sparkler, he ordered me below to fend off these boarders. Rushing down four-deck ladders to the main deck, I heard the ship's general alarm ringing direly and now found the chief officer and several deck hands dangerously cornered, fending off some forty or fifty of these invaders. In an inkling two of the pirates pressed the sixty-five year-old chief's back over the ship's rail, and within seconds, milliseconds really, he was about to be tossed overboard to a certain death. Either the small boats underneath would run him down, or his own ship's propellers would suck him in, chopping him to bits. I was about two steps away, and when I reached the beleaguered chief, a third boarder had also gotten to him. So I dispatched that third man with a single, well-aimed blow, propelling him over the side of the ship to the waters below. The other two pirates, realizing I was twice their size, tried to beat a hasty retreat, releasing the doomed chief officer. One of them felt his safest move was to hang over the side of the vessel, putting the rails between him and me, so I couldn't land a good swing or kick. But with the anger of revenge boiling over inside, I wasn't about to let him loose.

The thug ducked down, holding on for dear life, his hands clasped over the side of the scupper plate rising up from the ship's side, which he could conveniently grab onto with his fingers, staying low along the ship's hull—i.e., out of harm's way. He must have hoped I'd pass him by, in order to pursue his pals on deck. But I was so focused on the three guys who had attacked our chief officer that I didn't let him off the hook. I also feared he'd climb back up at an opportune moment, attacking me from the rear in a two-front war, which I wanted badly to avoid. So I clomped right over in heavy, steel-tipped boots, then proceeded to stomp off his fingers. As I was crushing them, he screamed, "No swim, no swim...." But I kept stomping, deciding not to consider his swimming ability, which he could soon test.

By now the rest of our crew had been roused out and we were engaged in hand to hand combat, outnumbered by probably two to one (they had fifty or sixty men to our thirty or so). Fortunately, we greatly outweighed and outsized these invaders, and by using dunnage and lumber on board, succeeded in repelling the boarders with little significant injury, but with considerable hurt and death on their side. Our casualties numbered perhaps ten or twelve of our guys cut and bruised, with one losing an eye; but at least we survived the attack!

That was my real baptism under fire, and from then on my days seemed to dawn in a different way. As calm and clear as it might be outside, my viewpoint had been permanently altered. I would henceforth be slow to trust people and situations, particularly in Third World settings.

This whole boarding episode had taken maybe a half hour from beginning to end, before I regained the ship's bridge. Throughout the invasion I had periodically heard gunshots from the bridge wing—the captain firing at the coxswain in the boats, or simply to put holes in their craft. After the episode I reported back to the bridge in a very anxious and nervous state, only to hear the captain say to me: "I'm going below, take over."

It took me several minutes to reorient the ship's position and survey impending traffic, collecting my thoughts with difficulty. I still had blood on my hands, feet, and everywhere in between, yet I kept thinking during the next two hours on watch just how lucky I had been. Only months later would I really focus on those who had died at my hands. This was primarily because episodes soon to take place would be equally traumatic, and paradoxically, curative for me. For within four days this now not so green third officer was about to experience one of the most unusual events he would ever encounter at sea.

It started on a tranquil morning out in the Bay of Bengal, a quiet, flat expanse of water that day, as we proceeded northwestward to the southeast coast of India and thence, to Madras. After a while I began feeling something unusual going on, for I hadn't seen the captain either at breakfast or on the bridge all morning. About eleven I heard a noise somewhat underfoot of me from the area of his cabin, sounding suspiciously like a gunshot. But I dismissed it as something strange I'd never heard on the ship before, presuming it to be a problem below decks, one the chief officer or other day workers would address. If they wanted me to know about it, they would surely call me on the phone to the bridge. Until twelve noon my duty was to navigate the ship—period.

Near midday the ship's second officer came up, as was his routine, to relieve me of my duties, allowing me to go down for lunch. His period for navigating would then last from twelve to four. En route to the lunch room I passed the captain's cabin, noticing his door closed, which also seemed unusual; but hunger exceeding my curiosity, I headed directly for the food.

After lunch I returned to the bridge to take a noon sighting with my sextant and was astonished to find only the second officer there. Historically in the maritime industry it was normal for a captain to take a noontime observation as well. I asked the second officer if he'd seen the "old man," and with surprise, the second officer replied that he hadn't. He called Crofton's cabin, but receiving no answer, presumed he might be eating lunch; but I indicated I hadn't seen him in the lunchroom either. Soon after, the chief officer came out to the bridge, asking if we had found Captain Crofton. We replied in the negative, then I asked the chief if on or around eleven he had heard a strange noise. Now I thought it might well have been the sound of a gunshot. The chief officer replied that he had indeed heard something, but was unsure what it was. He escorted me onto the bridge to continue our conversation out of the crew's earshot. After a brief discussion, he then ordered me to accompany him below to check further on the situation.

So we went to the captain's cabin and the chief, too, was surprised that his door was closed. He knocked, tried the handle, and realizing it was locked, walked around outside to have a look through the portholes; but the cabin's curtains were all drawn. He then decided to call the ship's chief engineer, and the three of us conducted a thorough search of the ship for our missing captain. Coming up empty, the chief officer next instructed the chief engineer to dismantle Crofton's door, but the engineer balked, pleading lack of authority for such a drastic move. The chief explained that the captain must be in his cabin and perhaps incapacitated. Therefore, the engineer had better follow the order to remove these door hinges at once and break in, an order duly executed.

The sight we beheld on entering the captain's office was truly a shocker. I was aghast looking through the office and the captain's stateroom, and seeing Sam Crofton's body lying in a large pool of blood next to him! The three of us stepped briefly into his cabin, and the chief officer told me to take his pulse. Detecting none, I realized he had sustained a severe wound to his head, since there was a hole in the top of it—and he was dead. The chief officer ordered me to stand back from the scene, and carefully making notes, he assessed the situation, wishing to preserve the scene intact for further investigation. We retreated from the supine body into the ship's office, where the chief officer noticed two handwritten letters lying on the captain's desk. Both were suicide notes the skipper had written, one to his former wife, one to a son in the Marine Corps stationed on Okinawa. The chief officer read the letters and with a look of disgust, said: "What a sorry end to a good man's life." There was also an unopened bottle of whisky on the table, with a third note in the captain's handwriting underneath, addressed to his personal steward and apologizing for the mess here. The bottle was a gift to him for having to clean up.

The chief engineer now requested permission to leave this ugly scene, but the chief officer ordered him and me to stay on as witnesses, until he himself decided to lock up and leave. The chief indicated we could not as yet find the ship's revolver. We weren't quite sure how the captain had done the deed, but in the shower there was blood and brains clinging to the overhead like stalactites in a cave. There was also a bullet hole in that area overhead. The chief officer now presumed that Crofton had placed the .38 in his mouth, pulled the trigger, and in his last, dying seconds, staggered out of the shower, falling into the stateroom. He ordered us not to touch or move the body. He then had the chief engineer, along with his support staff, reset the door, sealing it and locking it tight. The radio officer—or "Sparks," a common shipboard name—was then given instructions by the chief, henceforth the vessel's commander, to notify the shipping company of the disaster.

Our passage continued, and we never slowed down en route to Madras. What we still didn't know was the whereabouts of the ship's revolver, making the chief officer wonder about the exact cause of the captain's death—i.e., suicide vs. murder. However, evidence pointed strongly toward the former, based on Crofton's previous mental weaknesses displayed throughout the voyage—his constant reliance on others, and of course his bad nerves.

Having radioed the company, we received orders back the following morning, instructing us that since Crofton's ex-wife and his only son had no desire to claim the body, we should dispose of it in India according to local customs, and with proper documentation (official log entries conforming to U.S. maritime law). We were now approximately thirty-six hours from arrival at Madras on India's southeastern coast. Our voyage continued toward that port without incident, but there was quiet tension on board among crew and officers, and a general clouded aura covering the entire vessel. There certainly wasn't much conversation. Because too many officers knew the story of the captain's death and had leaked it to the crew, the chief gave up trying to keep it under wraps. Some speculated on a possible murder.

We made landfall off the lights of Madras harbor, but were unable to enter the harbor, since the ship wasn't yet given quarantine clearance. This angered the chief officer, because he wanted an immediate shoreside investigation undertaken by local authorities and the FBI. The following morning he instructed me to send a signal message to the shore station, requesting immediate permission for entry into the harbor, based on an unusually stressful situation on board ship. Request denied, the chief spewed out a stream of frustrated vulgarities. By now the captain's cabin was being invaded by numerous flies and other insects having at the blood and the rest, and it was apparent the chief officer wanted to resolve this matter quickly. So he handed me another handwritten message to transmit to shore station, clearly stating that he had every intention of heaving anchor and moving into the harbor, with or without permission. A return message indicated that in thirty minutes shoreside authorities would arrange for a berth, and our ship could then proceed into it.

An hour and a half later we were still awaiting further instructions from shore, so the incensed chief officer simply ordered the second officer and chief engineer to raise anchor and put steam on the engines. With this bold move, I saw for the first time what I considered to be a real captain in action.

As we approached the jetties, long rock fingers protruding into the ocean from the channel that goes in and out of the harbor, offering shelter to incoming ships, there was an urgent message transmitted to our signal message station, which I read and transcribed, then handed to the chief officer. It said: "Hold fast your position, do not enter the jetties, no berth is available, there is not sufficient room in the harbor for the vessel." The chief officer instructed me to send back a peremptory message—"Make room!" Pushing forward through the jetty entrances into the harbor, we dropped anchor amidst a cluster of ships. Authorities promptly swarmed aboard, cursing angrily in an Indian dialect—immigration people, customs officials, port authorities, police investigators, and others of all types and sizes. With a big smile our chief officer met them at the gangway, greeting them and taking them directly to the captain's cabin. To me he seemed cool under pressure, and I admired him for it. In fact I would have done anything he asked, being proud of his assertiveness at a time when the ship needed badly to be cleared of this problem.

A few hours later I was summoned to the captain's cabin, where I found local police or investigative authorities sitting in Crofton's business office, appearing and smelling drunk, with a bunch of empty and half-empty bottles of Scotch strewn about them. Flies remained thick on all surfaces, including on the still undisturbed body. About the same time a first FBI agent came on board, entering the cabin—a tall, thin fellow in his early thirties with sandy hair, and looking like an accountant. The agent got into a brief discussion with our chief officer, reviewing photos he had taken. Then in a quiet tone he asked the new captain what was going on here—he meant with all these drunks in the room. The chief officer replied: "I'm about to sweep them out, and that's why I called the third officer, who has a knack for being able to handle problems I'd rather not get involved in...." (One of those problems resolved included saving his life, but that was left unsaid.) The chief officer then raised his voice to local investigators, saying it was time to leave, and several still able to communicate grumbled about wanting to take unfinished bottles with them. At which point the chief officer told me to remove these guys from the cabin *now*; the party was over. I was happy to follow orders, quickly escorting the inebriated ashore, using support staff to carry them down the gangway to waiting water taxis, nothing more than broken-down, one-lung gas engine boats.

I then returned to the captain's cabin, and the chief officer and federal agent, informing me of their decision to move the body, asked me to stay on as a witness. They also told me to get in touch with the ship's bosun, assigning several seamen to bring up the stokeslitter, so that we could load the body into it. When the corpse was then lifted, the revolver was suddenly found in a pool of blood where it had lain under the captain. So much for that mystery...

As we positioned Crofton's hulk in the stokeslitter, I held his head under my hands, getting my closest look at him ever, and noting that the blood had poured through every orifice—nose, mouth, ear canals, and so on. That blood was dark brown to black, and now much dried or thickened. Crofton's eyes were totally red; there was no white left in them. And of course blood had also run down through the hole in the top of his head. I was ordered to have the gangway watch notify us when the steamship company agent's boat came alongside, because we were to lower the stokeslitter containing the body into the boat.

When that agent arrived, I met an unusual individual, one you couldn't forget. The man had nothing but a smile on his face, which from the outset was disturbing. I felt that under the circumstances he should have contained himself better. But by the end of the day that smile would be a welcome sight, because I was soon to do things I'd never dreamed of doing!

This agent notified me that I had been given the duty to record officially whatever occurred from the time of the body leaving the ship until its cremation. I was to note specific times of events, which would be subsequently entered into the official log, to be signed both by myself and the temporary captain.

These orders fell on my ears in a strange way, because I didn't know whether others had had to perform such duties on a ship. Most of the crew and officers were at least twenty years my senior. So I felt half like I was being given a stinking job and half like it was my obligation, accepting only because I was given orders.

The crew and myself carefully stowed Crofton's body into the boat at the end of the gangway, and glancing at one of his leather shoes, I observed that a hunk of cranial matter had fallen, and was dried and stuck on it. Gagging and almost vomiting, I restrained myself with difficulty. Once the body and stokeslitter were secured to the boat, I went down the gangway, joining the steamship agent to go ashore. There we were met by several people hired to help in the task of burial or body disposal.

We then loaded the stokeslitter onto a small truck (which in the British manner Indians called a "lorry"), boarded it ourselves, sitting in the back, and were jostled out into the countryside. I didn't know where we were headed, other than that steamship agent telling me about some cremation site. After a half hour of hitting what felt like every pothole in India, I could smell fires burning, and looking out from the back of the truck through the front windshield, observed several columns of black and gray smoke rising from an area a short distance ahead of us. As we approached, I could see an open crematorium site, where families were crowded around small pyramids of wood built as funeral pyres. These pyres ranged to the height of a small garage, maybe twelve to fifteen feet high, with all kinds of burnable debris stuck in through the center to fuel the fires.

Within seconds of arrival the body carriers had to separate Crofton from the stokeslitter and have his corpse dragged to the top of a funeral pyre. The "old man" was still clad in his captain's khakis and black leather shoes. For several minutes the steamship agent yammered with a group of Indians on my left, and I was somewhat disturbed by his absence. I wanted this cremation to be over and done with. I then observed a number of procedural events going on nearby, ones that were new to me.

After a few minutes the steamship agent returned, informing me that we had a serious ceremonial problem on our hands. Before we could start the fire to cremate the captain, we had to locate someone to crush his skull with a hatchet. Dumbfounded, I asked what he meant, and he repeated that we had to macerate Crofton's skull! If this weren't done, during cremation the human head (due to bone matter wrapped around the soft tissue of the brain) would simply explode, like popcorn in a popper. Indicating that I didn't customarily carry the appropriate instrument, I suggested he deal with the problem without me.

The man went straight back to the group he had originally been talking with, then three or four of them came over—taking a break from their own cremation ceremony about fifty yards away. They brought along a silver hatchet, and after a brief discussion, decided that *I* could borrow this ancient ceremonial tool to satisfy religious exigencies. Swallowing hard, I gazed up at Crofton's body, thinking about the consequences of not complying, and remarked one last time that maybe we could avoid this procedure, given that Crofton had already ventilated his own head with the bullet hole. But the steamship agent, along with the zealous group now surrounding him, highly recommended I take care of the matter, since it was not only physically, but religiously necessary. I would later learn that in this particular sect the oldest son had to provide this service for his dead father or mother.

Queasy and reluctant, I climbed the funeral pyre, a good fifteen feet up; and with legs now astride the captain's body, I looked down at him with hatchet in hand. Somehow—I don't know how—I managed to direct a hard blow right through his skull. Not wanting to do the thing twice, I made sure the first one sufficed. As I brought the hatchet up, I noticed that blood had run down my hand, dark red, serumy stuff, and I tried to wipe it off on Crofton's clothes. But the crowd below shouted that I was not supposed to do that and that it was time to descend. Carefully, I crawled down from the pyre, and the neighbors who had lent me the mallet told me how proud they were to have helped me, and that it would be a great memory for them that the family's sacred instrument had been used to dispatch an American sea captain into the hereafter.

I'd about lost my stomach, blurting to the ever-smiling steamship agent a couple of choice words, to the effect that it was time to get this awful operation wrapped up. Whereupon a fire was lit, and I stood there making log entries in my notebook, noting some of the circumstances I've described here. After about forty-five minutes I departed the scene, leaving the captain's ashes forever on the subcontinent of India. Returning to the ship, I issued a report to the chief officer, which was transcribed in the official log along with my signature and the new captain's, forever to be kept in Washington, as all ship's logs are. And I began wondering what had led me into this trade in the first place!

Chapter 2

A Young Cadet's Progress
and Revolt

MAYBE it started with challenges to be overcome from the very outset of my life. I was born October 24, 1947 at Children's Hospital in Buffalo, and within weeks faced a serious problem—from the start I regurgitated all my food. The doctors were puzzled, and after about a month of watching me waste away, told my mother that she needed to prepare for the fact that I might not live. (I had two older brothers, but this would still have been devastating to her.)

That mother, Phillis Dickson, had been born on a "north country" dairy farm in Antwerp, New York in 1919. She experienced a difficult childhood, inasmuch as her own mother had died when she was six, and being the oldest of three daughters, she had to become a kind of surrogate mom herself. She was raised by her grandparents, including a grandmother confined to a wheelchair, so she took care of her younger sisters, rounding up cows to bring them into the barn on cold mornings, so gramps and field hands could milk them—in sum, she was a busy young lady. But at least the Depression added little to these difficulties, due to the farm's self-sufficiency.

Before marrying my father, my mother went through a couple of husbands, and difficult times. Both had violent moods and tendencies, but her first husband was killed in the war, and the second marriage ended after a short time in divorce. Each union, however, produced one male offspring.

At the end of the war my mother first met my father, Kenneth William Orton, who was then a produce manager for one of the A&P's in Buffalo. My father had been born in Kittanning, Pennsylvania in 1916. From a coal mining background (Scottish coalminers who had come to the States and kept working in the mines there), his family had lived a typically dirt-poor Appalachian existence, barely scratching out a living. My dad's education was limited to sixth grade, and at age twelve he started working in the mines. However, he was an intelligent guy, hardworking too, and soon, at the insistence of his father, he was impelled to get out of the mines to redirect his life for his own health and welfare. In his early to mid-teens he worked at odd jobs, including selling magazines and working part-time for A&P. About 1935, when he was nineteen or so, he contracted the dreaded disease of the time, polio, resulting in a permanent upper curvature of his spine, which gave him a mild hunchback's appearance. Upright he would have been a tall man of 6'2". But with his shirt off you'd see the disfigured lump in his upper back. This precluded war service for him, and he was lucky simply to be mobile and functional.

During the war years he joined the National Guard and was trained in the miltary service, but obviously he had to stay home. About 1940 he married, but after delivering one son, his wife died prematurely in her twenties (from a female disorder). My father's National Guard training was in the Buffalo area, where he had met his first wife and worked full-time for the A&P company. One day, while grocery shopping for herself and her two sons, my mother bumped into him. The two struck up a conversation and it became a weekly, then a semi-weekly occurrence, and led to more and more tête-à-têtes at the A&P, since they looked forward to each other's company. After the war ended, they married, combining households.

However, just prior to that marriage, my half-brother Kenneth Jr. was lost from the clan due to a bitter court battle—awarding full custody to my father's in-laws (his dead wife's mother and father). My father was saddened for years by this because he felt that his child had been stolen, and that the judge had been bribed in some form, given that those in-laws had money. This may or may not have been the case, but that was his feeling. Until Kenny Jr. was about eighteen and finally sought him out, my father was never even given visitation rights. Once they met, against the wishes of the grandparents, they became fast friends, and Kenny Jr. grew to love his dad. He also came to love us as a family, so much so that prior to his death in Vietnam in 1967, he named his first-born son after me, Lance Drew Orton.

Back to my uncertain beginnings: here I was in children's hospital, about six weeks old, all emaciated and ready to die! Then Doctor Alford, my mother's pediatrician, in conference with a surgeon named Dr. Butch, recommended a last- resort exploration of a possible constriction in the esophagus above the stomach, called pyloric stenosis. Surgery was scheduled immediately—a brand new procedure for the time—and after an operation of several hours, Dr. Butch came out, reporting to my mother that the problem was now resolved and that "you'll never be able to fill this kid up again." Which, in fact, turned out to be true. I fulfilled the doctor's prophecy by having a solid appetite the rest of my life to date.

We were raised on Buffalo's East Side, when there was already dramatic racial turmoil and tension (early '50s), starting a pattern in my childhood of being always alert for possible altercations with street bullies. Mostly those fights involved blacks versus whites, real turf wars, though not of the gang variety, just neighborhood conflicts. "Don't walk on my sidewalk, or I'll punch your lights out" kind of thing... Watching my older brothers handle themselves, it became second-nature for me to learn the posture connoting toughness—at least that much was necessary to survive. In many cases this "look" sufficed to avoid conflicts, though nowadays such a tough guy act would be regarded as a joke. But I did get in fights, too, learning that I was able to defend myself, and in almost all cases, could neutralize my opponents. I don't ever remember really getting my butt kicked. My goal wasn't to inflict severe harm, just to overpower an attacker. Sadly, those fair fights would become outmoded, but that's how kids did things then. As I got older, the conflicts grew more violent, and I saw my older brothers in them as well, so I was on a learning curve upward. Or downward...

My parents recognized the fact that if their children continued to live in this deteriorating social atmosphere near "the Rockpile" (formerly called Civic Stadium), that we'd probably grow up to be criminals. Buffalo's West Side, mostly Italian, was more stable then, where the East Side wasn't—it was a volatile mixture of Polish, English, some German, and African-Americans, each group with its own enclaves. The South Side contained the Irish, while North Buffalo had Jews—a good neighborhood.

Anyway, my parents figured we should skip out to the suburbs, so around 1955 we joined the gold rush, moving to the town of Tonawanda, not really that far from downtown Buffalo by today's standards, but in that era, a new, safe neighborhood with nothing but fields, woods, and a *lot* of mud. My mother, the laundress, would come to know that mud very well.

With a family that included a younger brother named Drew, born in 1949, and who would follow me to the Maritime Academy, things quieted down. In Tonawanda I became—except for our long, aforementioned car trips in summer—a somewhat typical suburban, church-going kid (Lutheran). It was a period when most everyone regularly attended church or synagogue, and I was a believer, a church-going participant not by election, but by command. My parents simply left me no alternative, until later in life, when I made my own personal choices about religion.

In my early high school days I loved athletics, initially football, then swimming, which became my big competitive sport. In summers, like all American boys of that generation, we spent days playing baseball on sandlot fields; or on unusually hot ones we'd walk to the Lincoln Park municipal pool to aggravate the lifeguards, until frequently one of us got ejected, and the rest then left, too. In the fall we played touch football on the streets or in the schoolyard.

But swimming became my focus in high school, especially endurance events, 200 and 400-yard freestyle. In the summer of 1965 I graduated from Kenmore East High School, and then entered college. My swimming ability had improved to the point where at SUNY New York Maritime College in Fort Schyler (Bronx), I would break every freestyle record the school had posted—as a freshman! Not only in distance events, but in sprints. This engendered a kind of celebrity status there that would work both for and against me.

What made me choose this college? My main reason was its offerings for a potential degree in oceanography. I always seemed to have this thing about water—I loved to swim in it, and at least in my mind, thought I'd love to navigate on it, too. Somebody once told me that Scorpio is a water sign, and I was born under that sign, though I give little credence to such an explanation.

But to obtain a bachelor's degree in oceanography, I also had to undergo all the training and pressures of the military. As a freshman I soon learned that upper classmen called us mug cadets, and I rapidly concluded that I should distance myself at all costs from them. Some, particularly those who must have had severe insecurities stemming from their home lives, enjoyed bullying the underclass by issuing them demerits, which required extra duties. In some cases they eventually caused mugs to be ejected from the academy. One thing you didn't want to get here was the label of being a troublemaker or backtalker to upperclassmen—a surefire kiss of death. Which is how my celebrity status created problems, since a mug's best position was to remain an unknown. There was something of a predator-prey mentality here, and you helped ensure your survival by escaping notice. I should add that the ejection rate during the first year ran to at least 50% during that period.

Because I was so known as a swimmer, my only hope for survival was to put together a kind of protectorate of other upperclassmen, ones with athletic ability and interest, who would hopefully restrain their more predatory classmates and keep me from getting demerits. This worked quite well, and I managed to survive my first year relatively unscathed.

Just prior to going off to college, however, a tragedy had occurred in my family. In June my father passed away unexpectedly from a heart attack, only a few weeks before my high school graduation. I still remember how my own heart sank as I walked across the stage to receive a diploma, knowing my father would have wanted to be there. He was a good dad, a very good one, and he had adopted my older brothers. When he passed away, my oldest brother Paul seemed to be having a difficult time, because he had truly "adopted" my father as well. But I didn't take this death lightly either, though I showed less emotion. The timing was slightly easier for me than for the others, insofar as I'd soon be under such pressure at college, and so focused on daily survival that I had almost no time to mourn.

I was never a straight A student either in high school or college; instead I was about an average C+ student, though I excelled in certain areas, such as high school history, and in college subjects like military sciences, navigation, and really, all maritime-related areas, which surprised me. It seemed to be something inside me that I had never known was there. I just grasped it all, comprehending things about ships before I had even set foot on them!

But my college years *were* stress-filled. First of all, this was a full-time experience, for instruction went on even in summer, with actual shipboard training. Each year culminated with these summer shipboard training crews, testing our classroom experience gleaned that year. From a semester point of view, we usually never carried less than twenty-three or twenty-four credit hours, which along with the demands of military training, made for a tougher schedule than most undergraduates today must experience. And in that era, as noted, you could easily flunk out, even if the upperclassmen didn't succeed in destroying you first.

Some of my weaknesses in the classroom included the more arcanely technical parts of electrical training; college physics, a nightmare; and foreign language courses (French, and a smorgasbord of superficial greetings and other phrases in several languages the Academy believed would be useful abroad). In fact, it turned out that all maritime business worldwide is conducted in English, except up in the Shetland Islands, where they swear they're speaking English, but it's Gaelic to me!

There were several incidents in those years that did start to season me as an independent thinker and adapter. My ability to restrain myself from taking violent action was certainly tested during this cadet period, with a portion of the upper class always ready to bait or berate you. It took a lot of self-restraint not to leap to their barbed hooks. But in one particular incident, where a bunch of us did lose control, several of my classmates were expelled permanently for retaliating against patent unfairness. This incident took place in summer on a training cruise, when an upperclassman falsely accused one of my classmates of sleeping on watch, probably the worst crime one could commit on a ship, outside of murder. We knew this was a bold-faced lie on the part of this upperclassman, who had a vendetta going with our friend and classmate, Mike Bozzone. Mike and the rest of us always tried to control our tempers, but in this case, Bozzone was being charged with dereliction of duty, which if it brought a conviction by the sole word and witness of the upperclassman in a captain's hearing, meant instant expulsion.

The supposed incident and ensuing accusation took place during a nightwatch, and within minutes of the time we became aware of it in the wee hours of morning, nine of us plotted to retaliate. As mug cadets our sleeping quarters were located in the deep cargo hold of the ship, where we formulated our plan. Quietly refraining from waking some of our fellow classmates, we decided the best way to fight back was to urinate in a bucket, then in a carefully planned foray to the upper decks, carry the bucket into the upperclassman's room, where he would be sleeping alone. We would then hopefully douse him with the concoction!

After all the conspirators had urinated into the bucket and it was half full, lookouts were posted, and we carefully, but speedily transported the reeking brew from the lower hold to the upper deck area, where the accuser slept comfortably under his sheets. All this doubtless sounds like a gross thing to do, but by that point in the voyage we were all worn out, which of course does not justify such an ugly deed. But having been under the physical duress of long watches and heavy study schedules, and also working at maintenance and repair duty on board ship, sleep was never anything but a luxury. I guess our nerves must have been frayed.

So in one quick maneuver we flung open the guy's door, rushing inside in the dark, and throwing the bucket of stinky liquid all over him, along with his bedclothing, bunksheets, and mattress, splattering it everywhere. We had exacted our revenge, but news of the event would obviously anger much of the upperclass, as well as the ship's officers and captain.

The following morning at about 9:30 my entire class of approximately 300 was summoned to the mess hall, where several of the more militant upperclassmen, backed by the ship's officers, began a grim verbal interrogation, trying to learn who was responsible for the incident of the previous night. They demanded heads, though there were no witnesses to identify actual participants.

These militant upperclassmen, a minority who relished their authority, were minions of the administration and ship's officers, though some of the latter were decent men. But there was a faction of officers that was all spit and polish, reminding me of Nazi S.S., not of people who might teach cadets anything regarding virtue, etc. When these upper class minions found they couldn't extract any confessions from the entire class, they began a physical inquisition, requiring us to stand at rigid braces, a position where one had to extend the chest outward and one's chin as far down as possible onto the chest, and with arms and legs perfectly straight—in a rigid, muscle-straining position. Bracing someone up for more than five or ten minutes is clearly sadistic, as it becomes most uncomfortable for the victim.

There were other tortures they would inflict on individuals, such as making them sit in the "green chair." If they interrogated someone and didn't like the answer, or didn't get a response, militants would order underclass cadets to sit in this "green chair," which in fact was no chair at all. It was simply a position you had to stay in, bending your knees as though you *were* in a sitting position—but with no support whatsoever, until your leg muscles gave out and you fell down on the deck. Which then brought gales of laughter, and was frequently followed by orders to do push-ups and sit-ups, hopefully producing a confession.

We spent a long portion of the day being tormented in this manner, until that evening the ship's captain came down and dismissed the upper class, then tried in a more conciliatory way to extract oral confessions of those who might have been responsible for the bucket-of-pee incident. The room was deathly silent; one rule that every classmate always tried to maintain was never, ever to rat out a buddy. So we all hung together. Just prior to the evening meal the captain finally dismissed us, and that was the last we would see of him until a later date.

About seven p.m. I was called to officers' quarters and told to wear my white dress uniform, which was stifling in the humid heat. There I saw a line of about ten or twelve cadets, several of whom were my co-conspirators. The minions were there, too, maintaining a brace line of cadets, and one at a time the cadets were being called into an office, whence I thought I detected (through the door) the voice of one Colonel Pilosi.[2] About an hour into my wait one of my upper class friends, Bob Ratcliff, a fine person, came by, and without really stopping, but at a slow walk, told me quickly, "Don't confess to anything." Then he kept on walking. He had spoken while his more extreme cohorts were momentarily out of earshot. I got the impression that their absence was not haphazard, but forced on them by more moderate classmates, giving Bob a moment to speak with me. My friend Dick Corso stood beside me and he must have heard the comment as well.

Finally, after some time, it was my turn to step into the small mailroom being used by Pilosi as an extremely tight-quartered interrogation office. It was no bigger than eight by eight, but with enough room for him to sit in a chair, which he was doing in a sleeveless teeshirt. The temperature in there had to be 100 degrees. Colonel Pilosi became our main inquisitioner, probably appointed by the captain after his inability to break us down, but a job Pilosi would have gleefully assumed anyway. It was a good guy/bad guy routine—since the good guy couldn't wring out a confession, the bad guy now had his shot. I was surprised to see Pilosi out of uniform, as he was always spotless in appearance and the true image (in my mind) of an S.S. officer. I realize this is probably an unfair, even frivolous analogy, but that's the way I saw it at the time. Things seemed dire; for if I were kicked out of this institution, I would truly have considered my world at an end, facing, as I did, the extraordinary pressure of trying to become the family's first male ever to graduate from college. I also wanted to do it for the sake of my recently deceased father and for my mother, who was then suffering from terminal cancer, just recently diagnosed.

Through a number of interviews and police state-type interrogations, several of my co-conspirators were reluctantly impelled to confess. I, too, was threatened big time by Pilosi, and he promised that if I came clean, he would make sure that I remained in school.

Let me re-emphasize that this interrogation took place in a very small room, not much more than the size of a kitchen table. Pilosi barely had room to sit there in his sleeveless undershirt and khaki pants. But when I was called in, *I* had to be clad in heavy winter garb—and the heat was unbearable. I was told to stand at a brace, the first time I'd ever seen an officer do this to a cadet, or even heard of it happening. From the upperclassmen, yes, hazing was par for the course—

---

[2]   This is a pseudonym.

but not from an officer. When Pilosi ordered me to stand at a brace, it furthered fueled my anger, now growing to a white hot point, because I could see that these officers were totally out of touch with the pressures that the voyage had placed on us, and had accepted without question the upperclassmen's accusations against my friend. I felt that I'd lost all my rights, and was just a cornered rat, being kicked at by Pilosi. I was simply furious that they would abuse me like this.

But somehow my self-esteem rose to the occasion, helping me survive this inquisitory cauldron. If it weren't for that self-esteem I had derived from somewhere—maybe because I was successful in swimming, or from what my parents had taught me—I would have succumbed. These procedures went beyond the limit of human decency, not that throwing a bucket of urine on someone is the way to go either....

For well over an hour I endured Pilosi's interrogation, denying over and over that I had any knowledge of the incident. He repeatedly threatened that unless I confessed, I'd be thrown out of school. Finally the colonel jumped out of his chair, and nose to nose, screamed at me with garlic-laden breath that they had witnesses and would produce them at my court martial, so things would go easier for me if I simply came clean! At that point I couldn't hold back any longer, and responding in a voice that could surely be heard through the closed door and out into the hallway, I yelled: "Then bring on those sons of bitches and have them testify against me at Captain's Mast!" (A shipboard hearing where the captain decides whether to find someone guilty of charges, and what sentence to hand out.) "I want to see their faces when they point the finger at their classmates!" I continued in the same forceful manner. With that, Pilosi's own face turned beet red. I didn't hesitate or flinch, as he slumped back into his chair, screaming in a loud, angry voice: "Get out!" He had one of the upper class minions take me away, then came a cry of "Next!..."

Within hours we learned that seven of the nine co-conspirators were to be ejected from school, that is, as soon as our ship returned to the U.S. (All this of course was taking place on the high seas.) It had been a real Gestapo-type operation. During my interrogation, the entire class was being worked over physically via sit-ups and push-ups, at the instruction and glee of some of the upperclassmen. It had been nice to see a few who came by, exhorting us quietly to stand firm. Had it not been for those words of encouragement I'm sure things would have been worse. I knew it wouldn't have bothered the spit-and-polish S.S. faction of upperclassmen one bit to see an underclassman thrown out of school, with or without justifiable cause; in fact, it probably gave real enjoyment to those who were abnormally power-hungry.

At least I knew that after this episode I would no longer be a mug cadet; that once we got back to school, I would myself begin to mount the ranks of the upper class, since on our return the new freshmen would be in the Academy. And I swore inside that I would treat everyone fairly to the best of my ability, regardless of rank or position, which may have been the most beneficial outcome of this whole episode.

The final result, however, needs to be underlined: of nine accused, seven *were* expelled. The two who survived the "bucket of pee" incident, heralded in the school's annals for years to come, were myself and Dick Corso. Dick and I had been fast friends before the incident, remaining that way until his untimely demise a number of years later (when as skipper of a ship, and apparently succumbing to work-related pressures, he was lost overboard). Dick remained a poor swimmer, though I spent much time teaching him at the pool in college. But lest one think that going over the side of a ship might lead to a second chance, even in warm water the probability of being recovered, and under the very best weather conditions, is perhaps 3% at best. In cold water you have no chance whatsoever, due to rapid lowering of body temperature—exactly the same as on the *Titanic*.

To survive Pilosi's interrogation I'd certainly played poker, responding in such a bold way to one of the Academy's senior officers. I'd somehow trusted that even though there were people who could testify against me, my classmates' integrity would remain intact, which proved true—i.e., that they wouldn't rat on each other. Those who confessed only confessed to their own individual deeds. And that alone saved Dick and myself from expulsion.

After this incident Corso and I bonded even more, and on vacations I'd go to his home in Maine, or he'd come to mine. Years later, after graduation, our families still visited each other, until he tragically lost his life. Dick was a sensitive guy and perhaps the most heavy-duty perfectionist I'd ever meet. Never happy with a grade, if he got 100, he'd want to figure out why he didn't get 101!

One interesting and ironic follow-up to the bucket of urine incident: by the end of a voyage, an award was given to the mug cadet showing the most aptitude for a career in the maritime industry. It was offered by the Gulf Oil company, whose sponsorship made available the sum of $500.00. Though highly unusual, the award that year was given to both me and Dick Corso, and we ended up splitting the money. But within hours after the award ceremony, I was called to Colonel Pilosi's stateroom, where he reminded me that it would still be his pleasant duty to see me expelled before I could graduate.

As the next years passed, I'd always look over my shoulder, carrying the stressful load of that warning inside. Many times, indeed, I did find Pilosi's shadow behind the scenes, trying to orchestrate some lie or false accusation against me.

One hour before my graduation ceremony, and with great satisfaction, I made a personal visit to the colonel while he was still in his office. Acting almost like a street thug, I walked into that office without authority or permission, pushing the door up against the stops in a loud manner, and approaching the edge of his desk in my full-dress ceremonial whites, looking down at the bald-headed bastard. His own shirt was impeccably starched and pressed tightly against his neck. And I said to him: "You've got one hour to do your deed, Pilosi." Then I added something like "I'll piss on your grave, you cowardly S.O.B.!" Of course I was careful to see that there were no witnesses around, before making my exit from his office.

With this bit of revenge extracted, I felt that I had finally conquered the man, mentally flushing him out of my system. Now I could triumphantly enjoy the graduation an hour later, when I received my diploma, and my mother in severely weakened condition came to see me graduate. She had always wanted to be there to witness the first in the family to receive a college degree. And I can tell you that I certainly wanted to please my mother, that is, while I still could....

Chapter 3

First Voyage to India

WITHIN a day of graduation and my entry into the Merchant Marine, I was called by a shipping agent down in Philadelphia and told that he had a berth arranged for me on board a tanker leaving for India. The ship's name was the *Vantage Venture*, an expanded, jumbo-sized, World War II-era T-2 tanker. This was to be my first maritime experience on my own, testing my education and giving me a flavor of what life would be like for years to come.

Arriving in Philadelphia the next morning, I met the steamship agent, and proceeded down to join the ship. After boarding the vessel, I met the captain, explaining briefly that this was my first trip to sea with a licensed officer, and that I might have questions about operations and procedures that were obviously new to me. A Greek man with olive color skin, he seemed very easy-going about the fact that he had a young, inexperienced officer on board, responsible for ship's navigation and safety eight hours a day. Welcoming me with kind words, he told me not to be overly concerned—things would work out. But I remained apprehensive.

We loaded cargo at several docks in the Philadelphia area—different grades of lube oil—and departed about a week later from the Delaware Capes for the open sea. I was surprised to find out that at twenty-one I was the youngest man on board. Nearest to me in age was a fellow of twenty-six, but under my direct supervision. Most of the others were in their thirties and up.

The weather was fair for the voyage, as we struck a course for the Cape Verde Islands off Africa's west coast, north of the Equator. There we were to lay over for one night and bunker the ship—i.e., take on fuel for the engines. For several days in advance of our arrival there, my young ears couldn't help but hear the scuttlebutt on board, basically having to do with the attractions of women. It would obviously be common for sailing men to talk in a raw sexual fashion about this or that woman they fancied. Most were hardened prostitute and smut aficionados, and most didn't pass up many whorehouses. If they didn't contract VD a half dozen times in the course of their careers, they almost wouldn't consider themselves worthy sailors.

My upbringing in a Christian home made me dislike that kind of conversation, and I never participated. Especially after my first several voyages I wouldn't even permit that kind of talk around me. I came to feel that I didn't have to stoop to that level of existence, and if these men wanted to be lowlifes, that was their business. I had higher expectations of myself and my life directions.

On our arrival at the Cape Verde islands I witnessed some of their activities first hand, with guys tripping over themselves to get to the cathouses. After that, conversations all the way around the Cape of Good Hope dealt with sexual exploits and how they expected to outdo themselves in Bombay. Overhearing these conversations, I got an earful concerning things I'd never known of before.

But during the voyage I was worked very hard by the captain and kept plenty busy. My work hours were mornings from eight a.m. to twelve, and evenings from eight to midnight for navigation on the ship's bridge. Every afternoon from one to five I would also work on deck, where I repaired various kinds of lifesaving and firefighting equipment, including lifeboats—an area where I surpassed other crewmen in expertise. This was overtime work, so I earned money here that I'd never dreamt of making. In terms of income I almost felt like a Rockefeller or Kennedy! But each day I grew more exhausted from all the hours I was putting in, and on one occasion asked the captain for permission to sleep that afternoon, rather than work. Unexpectedly, he blew a fuse, ripping me up one side and down the other. Asking me sharply whether I was here as a passenger or to work, he told me that if I wanted any more overtime, I'd better not broach the subject of rest again. I promptly apologized, indicating I'd be on deck any time called, overtime or otherwise.

Some three weeks after leaving the port of Philadelphia, and at the height of the dry season, when it was unbearably hot, we arrived in Bombay. As soon as we docked, most of my subordinates raced ashore to take care of their erotic needs. At the end of the first day they returned with wondrous tales regarding who they had been with, at what clubs, etc. One particular crew member engaged me while I was on watch during offloading of cargo, trying to make me understand what I was missing. In a rather lengthy conversation he graphically described all the particulars of clubs he'd visited in the last day or two. He mentioned one place called "the Cages," which any traveler to Bombay would be aware of—a notorious open air market, where women were put in bamboo cages by their whoremasters, usually women themselves. These caged prostitutes had in almost every case worked previously in whorehouses or "clubs," often becoming infected, and thereby lessening their desirability for higher-paying clients. But they were still in a position where they might continue to have some value to the lower echelon of men, often diseased themselves, and who didn't mind hiring them for low prices. In other words you could go there and risk death for a little pleasure, and at little cost.

During my cadet days some of my classmates had visited other red-light districts—in European cities like Amsterdam, Antwerp, Copenhagen, and especially Hamburg. But I had never participated, feeling that I had enough self-worth not to pay for favors.

Why then did this surrealistic cage story draw my attention? I guess the idea of women kept captive against their will and being used for sexual exploits boggled my mind, making me hear out the deckhand's tale, something I wouldn't normally do. I guess I had to find out whether I was getting my leg pulled or not. So when I got off watch that afternoon, I hired a coolie to take me down to this notorious area, wanting to find out how true this sailor's description might be. And perhaps to see first-hand how low humanity could sink. Of course after a mere twenty minutes or so I did see that it was all true enough; and my heart went out to these poor women. Some were truly beautiful, but almost surely diseased. They ranged in age from the teens to fifty or so. The whole scene utterly amazed me. I stood there dumbfounded, for I'd always thought of women as creatures to be respected. To think of these females in the same light as my mother, my future wife, or any girlfriends I'd had was simply incomprehensible to me. So I just stood there, shaking my head in amazement.

I noticed that the cages were arranged in sections, with a series of handlers owning perhaps ten or twelve women each, and of course he or she (usually she) was the roving cash register. The men would negotiate deals with the handler, bartering for whatever woman they wanted. They'd haggle and fight back and forth on price, which was extremely embarrassing to me. After about a half hour the whole process had become so repugnant that I couldn't stand to remain in the vicinity, and I decided to regain the relative sanity of my ship and cabin.

There I felt melancholy, pondering what humanity was all about, for I'd never beheld anything like this in my life. It took some time to absorb and feel it all. I had left the scene behind physically, but not mentally or emotionally. I did, however, consider the experience a kind of favor to me, in that from then on I determined not to associate myself at any level with such debauchery. And I committed myself to taking a stand on this at some future time, once my insecurities regarding ship's operations were relatively mastered. Being a young upstart you could not announce such a thing, until you had proven to subordinates and superiors that you were a man of character, and until you had won them over in that way. You had to demonstrate your ability to navigate and to deal with other ship's problems, including violence, and show that you wouldn't back off from hard work. Once established in that venue, you gained credibility and respect, and only then could you challenge the thinking and morals of others.

The following day a tall, thin, well-dressed Indian man came on board our vessel. Clad in military-style khakis, well pressed and creased, he was a far cry from shipboard coolies lying about with rags on their heads and breech cloths on their backsides. The man introduced himself as the petroleum inspector and was about my size, or close. He asked me for shipboard assistance to draw samples and have them analyzed on shore for quality control purposes. We got into an interesting conversation, and to my surprise, I learned that he was a Christian, which few Indians were. The way we broached this subject related to my experience of the previous day, still fresh in my mind. I must have noted to this man how the cage experience was so contrary to my upbringing, and thus, a bridge to our respective religious beliefs was crossed.

This well-dressed man told me that once the samples were taken, I might be interested in hearing more about his life. So I invited him to the officers' ward room, and after I got off work, we had dinner there, talking for several hours. John had been born and raised in a Muslim home. His father had four wives—the polygamous limit for Muslims— and a couple dozen children as a composite total from these women. The other, competitive wives hated his mother, since she was considerably younger than they were. John explained that he had one full-blooded brother, and that when they were young, his mother had persuaded his father that her sons should be educated in the local convent by nuns. This Catholic school constituted the area's best available education, but John's father only reluctantly permitted such a school choice, for it was not favorably viewed by Muslims. As long as the boys didn't convert, they would at least receive a good education. And because their mother was young and beautiful, she had obviously been able to prevail on an obdurate father's heart. The proviso was of course that they remain Muslims and *not* convert to Christianity.

None of the other children were permitted to attend this school, creating from then on a divisive, tension-filled family atmosphere. John's half-brothers and sisters became very jealous, and the boys' mother was also berated constantly by the other wives and given more menial jobs, while their father simply distanced himself from all this intra-spousal bickering. As well, there was constant vying for position in terms of inheritance. Even before the children were teenagers, these inheritance battles had already become acute concerning just who would get what; now they grew even more intense.

At about age fourteen John informed his brother, one year his senior, that he planned on converting to Catholicism. With great excitement and joy his older brother indicated that that was his desire as well. They knew the plan would not be well regarded at home, so they told only their mother about it. She immediately became hysterical, trying to explain to them what this ultimately meant—their death sentence! She noted that their father had been generous concerning their education, but had frequently warned them that if they ever converted he would have them killed.

So for several months the boys contained their enthusiasm about embracing a new faith, placating their mother by avoiding conversations with anyone else about these plans. John told me that his mother constantly begged them to reconsider, but the brothers were itching to leave the nest as Christians. At about fifteen and sixteen respectively, they finally went to their father—this was roughly seven months later—and informed him of their impending conversion. John remembered that father sitting quietly and listening, and then, when they had finished, standing up, announcing that he had disinherited them and would never see them again! He then called in his other children and all four wives, and in front of them, denounced these wayward sons. He declared emphatically that no one should speak to them ever again, that they should never be brought up even in conversation, and that the curse of Allah was henceforth upon them, i.e., a death sentence. Their mother began sobbing, beseeching her husband for mercy, but he ignored her pleas. She herself was interrogated on her faith, but tearfully assured him that she would remain a loyal Muslim. Her husband then announced that she would be allowed to live in his house and he would provide food for her, but she would receive no inheritance.

Then the boys were dismissed, thrown bodily from the home by the older brothers. After leaving, they weren't quite sure where to stay or what to do, so they walked back down this elevated dike roadway about four miles to the convent, where they knew the sisters would look after them (some Indian, some from the West).

The brothers stayed there and periodically, would leave the convent to do errands for the nuns, going to market, and so forth. On one particular trip they were returning along this extended dike, loaded down with items from the market; and suddenly, they were set upon by six to seven men and beaten to a pulp with clubs. In that group of attackers they recognized one of their older brothers. The thugs beat the boys unconscious, leaving them to expire there. John then remembered waking in the morning to see his unconscious brother lying in a pool of blood beside him, with birds picking away at his face and body. John himself swirled in and out of consciousness for three or four more hours. With difficulty he was finally able to maintain a conscious state, dragging himself away from the scene. He had a broken ankle and numerous broken bones, as well as contusions from head to foot. His eyes were swollen shut, so that he could barely see where he was stumbling. He continued bleeding profusely from different spots on his battered body. Several passers-by saw him and wouldn't help; apparently the village had put the word out, and as a result, these converts were considered lower than untouchables in the Hindu religion.

About a mile from the convent one of the sisters fortunately ran into John and he received assistance. They returned to find his brother, still miraculously alive, and brought him to the convent, too. After several months of convalescence both somehow survived the ordeal. There came a day toward the end of that recuperation when John's brother spoke about recanting his Christian conversion; whereupon John decided that no matter what his brother decided, he was going to continue in the faith he had chosen.

When his brother had recovered sufficiently, he returned to his father, asking forgiveness. Somehow he received it, and as far as John could ascertain, was reinstated in the family. But John never saw that family again. He only heard that his brother was OK, and that the family had taken him back (his sisters being the most tolerant and forgiving).

John, meanwhile, would get married, raise good children, and became a successful man. He was educated in every sense of the word, and he carried himself well.

One can imagine the mind of this twenty-one-year old American, having seen the "cages" only a few days earlier, now listening to this hair-raising account, and the thoughts going through his head at the time. In the cage operation I had seen the cesspool, the nadir of humanity, then met a man probably no older than thirty who had suffered so much at the hands of other human beings called family. It offered me interesting perspectives on life, teaching me that there was much beyond my comprehension going on in this world. Yes, I was beginning to be let loose from the cocoon in which I'd been raised, and in fact, my previous world began to seem banal; despite the heartless behavior I had endured in my cadet days, *this* level of heartlessness exceeded my usual powers of understanding. I made every effort to remain sensitive, but I also toughened my hide—trying to become more aware of the kinds of human animals that inhabit our planet. I suppose voyages to sea or to far-off lands had always modified prejudices, opened new horizons, and induced such intellectual and emotional changes in seafaring men.

I should add that in addition to these two encounters on my first voyage to India, I learned as well from being subjected on a daily basis to the poor, who would beg for literally anything. By the time we left India, I had given away almost all the clothes I owned, every bar of soap, and really anything I could hand over to help relieve the omnipresent misery I saw there, knowing that once back at sea I could buy necessities I needed from the ship's stores. Education doesn't occur only in classrooms, and in India I had taken quite a course!

Chapter 4

Strafing in Vietnam and American Rage

AS part of my military obligation to the U.S. Navy, I was required to travel in this era on merchant vessels with itineraries and ports of call in war theaters. The commission I had received as U.S. navy ensign was predicated on the fact that I had to sail ten months a year for three years, including on ships that might take equipment or supplies to Vietnam. But it was difficult to find sufficient deck officer staff to man such vessels. Most U.S. merchant marine officers avoided sailing on ships that entered a war zone, even though receiving an automatic 100% pay increase for being there. If the vessel came under attack, which was almost a foregone conclusion, there were additional bonuses that merchant officers would receive, that is, if they lived to collect them. The status of the U.S. Merchant Marine during the Vietnam War differed from that of World War II, when all merchant ships had basically been confiscated and operated by the government's War Department, similar to a situation today, where if a policeman needs to use it, under current civil law he can commandeer your car.

During the Vietnam War this was not the case, and thus merchant marine officers could select whatever ships they wanted, which left those traveling to Vietnam generally undermanned. It was not uncommon to find the dregs of maritime society sailing these vessels, because they couldn't find jobs with companies who had scheduled service beyond Vietnamese ports. To say the least, this situation presented a rather distorted picture of humanity on ships during my initial years at sea.

At one point on a trip to Vietnam, we arrived at Vung Tau, a port situated at the mouth of the Saigon River in the Mekong Delta area. After a couple days of waiting, a convoy of some fourteen ships was formed, and starting in the early morning, we made an eight-hour transit up river to the port of Saigon. This trip was quite an experience for me, in that surrounding terrain from the edge of the water up to higher ground at a distance of at least a mile was stripped of all vegetation. The ground resembled moon-pocked landscape, and at first I was perplexed; but it didn't take me long to realize that it was from strafing and bombing. The total lack of vegetation still made me curious, and I later found out that it was because the Americans regularly used Agent Orange to defoliate here. Planes would fly along riverine areas, spraying profusely to eradicate potential cover for the Viet Cong. Which of course didn't prevent the enemy from burrowing into these mud flats during the night, armed with rocket launchers and other light artillery. They would wait for the morning convoys to sail up river, on which they would then take potshots, strafing the ships. The usual target was a ship's bridge, because with their type of weapons—so light in nature—they couldn't do fatal damage to the ship itself. In some instances, especially if it were an ammunitions vessel, a huge fireball could be created and the ship might perhaps be lost; but for the most part the VC's goal was to kill crewmen navigating vessels upriver, firing anti-personnel or fragmentation rockets into the bridge, which of course is the ship's navigation center, including for steering.

While in Vung Tau, preparing for our voyage up river, we were supplied with sandbags, which we used to build a protective berm around the ship's wheelhouse and bridge. Since we were on a merchant vessel, by law we were not allowed to carry permanent armaments, making us particularly vulnerable to even minimal attacks from small arms fire or rocket launchers. On the ship's bow and stern the military did place M-60 machine guns, designed primarily to prevent divers and/or boarders from approaching vessels. Air cover was theoretically available, too, during the transit up river, but on an as-needed basis. Which meant that after the VC initiated an attack, we would have to call and act as spotters for the planes in order for them to take out enemy positions. On this kind of ship I felt much like the lady at the circus who spreads her body on the wheel, allowing the blind guy to fling knives at her! It was certainly frustrating, not to mention scary, watching VC rockets pass ten or fifteen feet in front of your face, just missing the bridge. On many occasions of course the ship was hit, and in some instances we lost lives on board.

One episode was particularly gruesome and sad, when an engineering officer was in his cabin, and it took a rocket hit. The shell penetrated the outside bulkhead, i.e. the cabin wall, which normally caused an explosion inside the cabin; however, the projectile was a dud, succeeding only in punching a hole about four inches in diameter through the wall. However, the unfortunate officer happened to be standing with his head over the sink, brushing his teeth in a direct line where the dud came through the wall. So it killed him instantly, taking his head off.

Once our business was conducted in Saigon, we sailed northward to Qui Nhon, a coastal port in a harbor surrounded by a rugged enclave of mountains. In that port the ship could only be worked at the dock during daylight hours. With the arrival of nightfall we would have to put out to sea, because the area was so overrun with VC each night. We would hasten off the coast out of range of their attacks, and in the morning return, resuming discharge of our cargo. The dock was well fortified with bunkers and sandbags, because even in daytime it was not unusual to be interrupted by VC mortar rounds raining down on us. At all times we maintained constant vigilance for enemy divers, who given the opportunity, would place a satchel charge on the ship. This was usually a hand-held magnetic device with an explosive core, easy to attach to a vessel's hull and equipped with a short timer fuse, which in most cases probably didn't give even the divers time enough to get out of harm's way. Any debris we noticed in the water were continually strafed, either by our bow or stern machine guns. One always assumed that such debris might be concealing a diver below, using some kind of breathing apparatus. So logs, vegetation, and really anything floating in the water were considered hazardous to us and generally blown apart.

In addition to the use of machine guns, the deck officer was required at fifteen-minute intervals to throw a concussion grenade over the side of the ship. This was designed to crush any living creatures—divers again—who might somehow have escaped our machine guns. So during my rounds, while surveying cargo operations, I would deposit these grenades in the water on the port and starboard side of the vessel, at those intervals of a quarter of an hour.

One day late in the afternoon the top authorities there—port officials, the captain et al.—said they were going to step up the pace, attempting to finish unloading operations before nightfall, since we only had a little left to do. But by the time dusk had approached, it was obvious we were going to end up working well into the dark, in order to complete the discharge of our cargo.

About nine or nine-thirty p.m., lethal darkness having fallen, we started taking heavy mortar rounds alongside the dock in the water and on the ship, too. As third officer I immediately ordered a complete shutdown of the vessel, including cargo operations, and as was required of me, closed all doors and ports leading into the ship's living quarters. These were "dogged down" and made watertight, and once closed, no one was permitted to pass through them. Our primary obligation was to preserve the safety of ships' officers and crew, in the event of boarders or VC agents showing up. Though unable to see outside, several times we felt the ship shake from concussions in the water. The captain was up on the bridge, trying to arrange for port officials to let us leave the harbor, but we were in a tough spot, since the crew couldn't stand out on deck to let the lines go.

I myself was on the main deck inside the living quarters of the vessel, when suddenly I heard what I took to be a security breach, emanating from below. In the crew's quarters I heard shouting and screaming, and it sounded like pain was being inflicted. I also heard the clatter of feet running, and doors slamming. So I cautiously proceeded down a ladder to the area from where I thought this noise originated. I had heard no gunfire inside, so I still believed this was some kind of security breach, whereby VC invaders must be using clubs or knives on the crew. I only had a Colt .45 pistol on me, which I had drawn before starting down the ladder. As surreptitiously as possible, I peered down the passageway to the area whence I'd heard the commotion.

To my amazement I beheld two of our own crew members in a furious, life-and-death struggle with each other. With that I put the .45 back in my holster and ran right over to a scene that was pitiful and gory. One white fellow lay in a corner, half his body covered in blood from head to toes. With his right arm shattered and bone simply hanging out, he was crouched and begging the attacker, a frenzied black man standing above him, for mercy before what looked like an imminent kill. The black man was dressed in a pair of shorts and held a bloody knife in his hand, slashing without mercy at this poor guy.

Without hesitation I came up from behind the slasher, reached out and grabbed him, while at the same time announcing that I was the ship's third officer. But before I could even get the words out—"I'm the third officer"—the man wheeled around with knife flashing, and I leapt backwards, feeling the wind of swirling steel whoosh by my throat. Had I been two inches closer he would certainly have slit my jugular, and killed me. The man's eyes were bloodshot red and hysterical—they kept flying left and right in the sockets. Everything told me that this dude was overdosed on something very bad. In about a millisecond I had to make a decision as to whether he really knew who I was, and whether or not he would take orders from me.

So I blurted out, "Drop the knife, I'm the third officer!" With that he stared at me with a cold, vacant look—so much for orders. By taking one step back I had probably made the first mistake in this confrontation. Now he took a deliberate step forward, holding his knife about chest high and pointing it directly at me, his new prey. I tried to maintain a safe distance, but taking another step forward, he closed that gap. Again, I retreated a step, and as his foot started off the floor toward me once more, I turned and ran, out of a primal sense of self-preservation. The layout of that living quarter area was made up of four interconnecting corridors, forming a rectangle. At that point I began running down one short corridor and on reaching the port side, hurried down the length of that corridor, till I could go no further. I then ran across another corridor over to the long starboard quarter, with the crazed attacker following in hot pursuit.

Having forgotten I had a .45 on my hip, given that .45's weren't normal issue, except in Vietnam, and even then only for certain officers; and not yet understanding that crew members could be enemies, I completed one lap around to the original spot, where the initial victim had now managed to gather himself up and was able to hide behind better cover—spare boxes and other stuff in the passageway. I didn't spend much time checking on his new position. In fact, I almost hoped my passionate pursuer would stop and concentrate on his first victim, allowing me to mount a more aggressive rear assault. However, that didn't occur, and I started lap number two. This second go-around bought no more space between the two of us; actually a lot less. My pursuer was fleet of foot and I'd never been known to be that fast on my own. But during the race I had had the presence of mind to notice a fire axe hanging on the bulkhead, which I had just passed on a lap. So with an extra effort, knowing my survival depended upon it, I raced into lap number three, determined to gain enough space and time to pull the fire axe from the bulkhead and confront my pursuer with it. To do this I ran harder and faster than any Olympic champion—or so it felt. Amazing what surges of adrenalin can engender in a human...

Having reached the fire axe's location, I reached out in a single motion, grabbed the handle up close to the head, yanked at it, and fortunately, the damn thing came out clean. Now I turned and pivoted with the fire axe, in full view of this crazed attacker. My fear began to dissipate like a San Francisco fog, replaced by furious anger welling up from deep inside. My feet wouldn't retreat a further inch, and with cold-blooded hatred impelling me, I prepared to blitz my attacker with the fire axe. Kill or be killed was the message in the air. However, because of the speed and lack of time with which I'd gotten hold of the axe, the head was under my two clenched fists. Which from a practical point of view turned out to be beneficial, because I now had a proper weight fulcrum, allowing me to give repeated blows to my attacker. If I had been holding the ax by the end of the handle, I probably would have gotten only one clear chop at him. So instead of having a cutting device, I had a *beating* device—a kind of club in my hands. I should add that fire axes are made of hard ash, for which I'm still grateful. As I lunged toward the manic seaman, he stopped momentarily. But I was coming on like a freight train with no brakes, and steam and fire had to be pouring out of me like I was crazier than my attacker—which I probably was at that moment. He might have been high on illicit drugs, but I was high on endorphins or adrenaline.

When I got to him, he brought up his right knife hand, obviously intending to rip me to shreds. However, by using a cross body blow across his head to his shoulder and arm, I landed the first whack of my club. The handle glanced off his skull and went down hard on his left shoulder blade. His knife had reached my left breast, never having been able to cross my chest, but he did cut me in my left pectoral. In the heat of conflict I never felt it. Within seconds I struck several more blows on my assailant's head and arms, until I could see he was totally incapacitated. His knife fell to the ground and he lay there moaning, next to his original victim. Several of his teeth were shattered, his nose was broken, and his whole right side had been well bruised (i.e., his attack-hand side).

In addition to all this torment, the heat was simply intolerable. Closed in due to the VC attacks and without ventilation, we had been fighting in an oven-like atmosphere of a good 100 degrees. That heat and the feeling of being cornered helped make the situation as intense as it was. Shaken, I kept wondering what I would have done if I hadn't noticed the fire axe. At some point, and not much further—for I was about out of laps—I would have turned on the guy, but he was very strong, with a body of glistening, rock-hard muscles. I realized that if it had just been straight-up fighting, I would have had less than a fifty-fifty chance.

Shortly after I regained some mental composure, the captain and several other crew members approached the scene, asking what had taken place. To the best of my ability, though still shaken, I tried to describe the episode. A search of the attacker's cabin found that he had in fact purchased narcotics from dealers on shore—a variety of drugs—and had obviously decided to test his wares.

About this time the U.S. Navy gave us orders to depart the port, even while we were still under attack, and they also had to arrange hastily for hospitalization of these two injured men. So we sailed for

Da Nang, arriving the following morning, minus the two wounded crew members. Once in Da Nang the U.S. Coast Guard sent an investigation team to the ship in order to gather details on the previous night's episode. Since I knew I'd never see either of them again, I didn't think much of it. In fact, I quietly hoped the attacker would die, because I was still frustrated about his malicious attack on his victim, the result of drug-induced insanity.

The officer assigned to the duty of chief investigator held the rank of commander, which under the circumstances was pretty high up. Normally these kinds of proceedings are conducted by lower-ranking officers. After taking my statement and that of the ship's captain, he indicated the report would be sent back to the San Francisco office, and that based on facts he had received, I seemed to have taken actions appropriate for self-defense.

I thought nothing further of the incident, but three months later, after completing our voyage, which had continued eastward en route to Seattle, I got a big surprise. For as soon as we docked, a Coast Guard boarding party came onto the ship, consisting of a couple of investigators and other bureaucratic personnel. When they strode up the gangway, I happened to be on duty and asked them what their purpose was on our ship. They said they had to see the captain, regarding an incident that had occurred in Vietnam. It had something to do with an altercation on the vessel—one between the third officer and an engine room fireman. I never identified myself, so they had no idea with whom they were talking. Instead, I simply gave them directions to the captain's cabin and went about my duties. About a half hour later the captain sent word for me to report to his cabin, which I did, and there I saw the Coast Guard investigators, soon to become my inquisitioners!

I should add that these Coast Guard inspectors were both Lieutenant "J.G.'s," far beneath the rank of the original, and what I presumed to be the final, investigator. When questioning started, I remained surprised as to why the case was being reopened at all, when the Coast Guard commander in Vietnam had basically said it was a closed book. So I asked these investigators why they needed another deposition from me about the incident. Their answer was that they were simply following orders, and that the matter had somehow found its way to union officials, who had breathed new life into it by playing what we now call the race card. To follow orders these gentlemen had to take a second deposition, and they announced that I must remain in Seattle and probably face an administrative law court hearing there!

I was plainly angry, because I'd been gone several months, I was supposed to get my "relief" in Seattle, so I could go on vacation for three months, and now I was being told that on *my* vacation time and before returning home, I had to participate in a court room circus, justifying my actions in Vietnam. After giving my deposition, I learned that my assailant had survived the incident; however, he was permanently disabled and would probably never work again. I also learned that his first victim had recovered reasonably well, though with over 100 stitches and several broken bones.

The captain listened to all this incredulously, just shaking his head; he seemed quite frustrated, and as for me, I was openly seething at the resurrection of this incident. Noting my rising anger, the Coast Guard investigators cautioned me not to leave Seattle without informing them. They said I would be subpoenaed the following day for the hearing. After the Coast Guard personnel departed, the captain told me it would be a good idea to hang around and make sure I went to the hearing, because if I didn't, they could pull my license.

My relief arrived shortly thereafter, and I went down to the Coast Guard authorities to plead my case, hoping to persuade them to allow me to go home and testify through the Buffalo office. While in the Seattle office, however, I ran into a former classmate of mine, Gary Gales, who surprisingly acted civil and friendly to me. This astonished me, because during my college years Gales was the only classmate of mine with whom I'd ever gotten into a physical scrap. We were roommates at the time with another guy; and one day under the stress of exam preparation, he commented in our cabin that he didn't like the way I studied, and that it detracted from his own ability to cram. So Gary and the other roommate decided they were going to teach me a lesson. I'll never forget how Gales—only about 5'7" and maybe 140 pounds, where I was 6'4" and near 200—jumped on my back like a monkey. With him on my back the other guy came at me head on. Both agreed that I distracted them in their studies and to be fair, I *was* the type who only absorbed things by fidgeting, putting my feet up, then down, rising to pace, cleaning off tables, cracking knuckles, or moving my chair, while I pondered textbook content. Meanwhile, those two guys ingested their material like manikins, with noses stuck firmly in their books.

So here's Gary on my back and the other roommate, John Underhill, closer to my size, confronting me face to face, and I had to figure out how to raise my arms and defend myself, in case John threw a punch at me. So I decided to run backwards about six feet, with Gary clinging to me like a barnacle, and then I hurled myself against the wall, making Gary the ham in a painful sandwich. Gales had an explosive temper, probably exacerbated by being a rather short fellow. But having succeeded in mashing him and "debarnacalizing" myself, I knew he was no longer a problem—he was gasping for breath behind me and as I let loose, he crashed to the floor. When that happened, I bounced off the wall like a handball back toward John Underhill, who fled through the open door into the passageway, leaving black streaks on the linoleum from his well-shined shoes. I then turned around and helped Gary up, football-style, and down to the bathroom, where I gave him some wet paper towels with which he could wipe his forehead. I needed to keep him conscious. For several minutes or so he continued gasping for breath, and I thought I'd really hurt him. I was later happy to learn he had only suffered a bruised rib and probably a bruised ego as well.

Once John returned, we had a peaceable pow-wow about my study habits, and I decided I'd go elsewhere to cram. Henceforth, I proceeded to the library to liven things up a bit there, probably irritating the hell out of other cadets busy poring over their books. All in all, I was pretty well liked as a student, but one exception to that rule was this Gales fellow, whose ego and ribs I had bruised.

Bygones, however, now seemed to be bygones, and he informed me that he had gotten married and settled in the pretty city of Seattle. Perhaps we'd both grown up a bit; at all events I found his whole demeanor pleasant and quite likeable now. He asked me if I wanted to go home with him to Seattle's North End and have dinner and stay overnight, since I had to attend court the next day. I agreed, and for a few hours we enjoyed each other's company, winging up the freeway past all those green hills overlooking silvery lakes. When we arrived at his house, we inhaled a wonderful spaghetti dinner his new bride had prepared for us. We talked about old times, but for her sake I avoided discussion of once having smeared her husband against a wall! We spent an enjoyable evening together, and when it came time to retire, I was given the pull-out sofa. The following morning I looked out at the early fall, and off we went to the hearing—with Gary dropping me off downtown.

A panel of three judges was hearing the case, which surprised me. I wasn't surprised, however, to learn that I was being represented as the bad guy by the plaintiff's attorneys. The hearing would determine whether or not I had used excessive force, and that *did* flip me. You lived in a Darwinian world, you did what it took to survive, and suddenly your license to make a living hung in the balance? It all felt very unfair.

To further describe the scene, here was this now crippled black man in his early thirties sitting in a wheelchair, accompanied by union-provided attorneys. On the other side I was on trial without any real representation, except that of the Coast Guard, who weren't about to protect me. They were only there to follow whatever action the judges deemed necessary. Obviously naive, I simply couldn't fathom that they might take away my right to make a living after all the years I'd invested in school, then garnering my laurels as a seaman. The now crippled fellow and his attorneys got everyone sobbing at his sad, but distorted story. I couldn't believe that I didn't even have his original victim in court as a witness. May I digress a bit? It just seems to me that that was about when America began going corrupt, albeit that it was the supposedly idealistic age of hippies, protest, and extension of civil rights.

But where were *my* rights? My only means of defense was my own testimony, as well as the original commander's report, of which I had a copy. There he had stated that my actions had been totally justified. He also stated that it was an officer's duty to protect and defend all crew members on board as best he could. The plaintiff's attorneys argued that if that were the case, I had grievously erred in attacking their client, mercilessly beating him into this crippled state. They failed to mention anything about the man's drug-induced derangement, and the fact that he himself had already beaten a fellow crew member into a bloody pulp. Their scenario was that without obvious cause I had gone below decks, presuming that since the ship was under enemy attack, this poor black guy in difficulty was some kind of an intruder.

That of course was pure fiction, but it took about two hours of testimony on their part and about an hour on mine for the judges to render a decision. After a while I became very nervous, even considering that if they voted unjustly against me, I might just finish off the job at some future point. The whole charade angered me so deeply that I really struggled with that extreme thought. Fortunately, in a two to one vote they decided that I had acted in the best interests of crew and vessel, and that there was no validity to the claim that as third officer I had used excessive force in this incident. It was within my rights to act in any manner necessary to defend myself, even if that meant subduing an attacker in a violent manner.

Within an hour of the decision I was at Sea-Tac Airport, and six or eight hours later, back home in Buffalo with my bride of less than a year. Home, in other words, to see my Susie—petite and with strikingly beautiful features, a fair complexion, and dark black hair obviously inherited from a partly Native-American background.

Five months later I found out definitively what happened to both the deranged assailant and his first victim. I learned that the white guy recovered fully and subsequently returned to sea. As for the black man, our altercation, as I had seen, left him permanently disabled and unemployable in the Merchant Marine. I suppose I should have felt sorry for him, but I had been fighting for my own life!

Chapter 5

Enter the Divine Element

I N 1973 I applied for a position with Gulf Oil, having heard that they were hiring junior officers, and after the interview, they assigned to me one of their coastal tankers. To my surprise I ran into my old classmate and friend, Dick Corso, who was on the ship. He was a third officer here, and because this was my first voyage with Gulf and they didn't really know my expertise, I started out as junior third officer to Dick's senior third.

Within a few weeks Dick went on vacation, so I was tapped to fill in for him while he was gone. The captain and I got along well, and he gave me very good recommendations. After a few months I was promoted to second officer, or third in command on the ship.

Most of the company's ships ran Gulf Coast-East Coast operations, and while I was on vacation, the company called, asking me if I would join one of their vessels requiring additional help. Apparently the third officer on that ship was not working out well in his position, so they wanted me to assume his senior post, and he was bumped back to junior third. His name was Larry Raines[3], and for several weeks he resented me, feeling a victim of injustice, for which he blamed me. In fact, I had had nothing to do with his demotion. Eventually we talked it out, becoming if not bosom buddies, at least cordial acquaintances. From then on Larry took orders from me without any sneers or backtalk, and our working relationship went smoothly.

Word eventually came down from the captain that Larry was to be reassigned to another Gulf ship, headed to Alaska. But within a few weeks we received shocking news that this "Gulf Queen" had suffered a major complication during loading up there, and that the young officer I had just been sailing with, along with the vessel's second officer and captain, had all been gassed to death within a cargo tank. The only surviving officer on that ship was its chief officer. News of the Alaskan disaster further focused me on the dangerous line I was walking in my trade, as if I didn't realize it enough already. Such tragedies helped remind you of safety procedures, and of how much you needed to keep

---

[3]   This is a pseudonym.

your head during a crisis. And in fact these men *had* died due to an initial mistake, compounded by further errors others had made.

There but for the grace of God go I? You said it! For on January 5, 1975 I myself should have died—yes, I should have bought it. Not that there hadn't been and wouldn't be many other days in my life when I managed to escape harrowing maritime situations; but the incident I recount here was without doubt one where *all* involved knew their survival was plainly miraculous.   Fully loaded with different grades of gasoline—premium, aviation fuel, regular leaded, and other highly volatile hydrocarbons—we had left Texas, and our first stop was Port Everglades (Fort Lauderdale), where we discharged about half our cargo. From there we went north along the coast to Jacksonville, where on arrival at a sea buoy, thick fog had set in, which the area generally gets in winter.

I certainly expected the captain, whom I admired, to anchor our ship for safety reasons, proceeding no further up into the St. John's River. Our destination was Drummond Point, the site of the Gulf Oil terminal. It was about supper time when we arrived at the sea buoy, and the decision on whether to go up river, or to wait for the fog to lift was deferred. The captain and the pilot simply could not make that determination. I was happy to go and eat dinner, but when I came out afterward, I was surprised to see the ship moving, since it was still very foggy out. I went to my cabin, while the captain, chief officer, and pilot took the ship on its course.

Then, at precisely 6:18 p.m., January 5, 1975, the vessel was suddenly rocked by some huge impact on the starboard bow. It rolled heavily to port, and sitting in my cabin, I was jarred out of my chair earthquake-style—right onto the floor. It was apparent that this was some kind of catastrophic situation, as I could hear what sounded like four or five diesel engines from a locomotive, coupled with the horrendously loud noise of steel being crushed. It was evident we had been struck by another ship and were in a bad, cataclysmic collision. Before my eyes I fully expected to see the imminent flash of a large fireball explosion, ending my life.

The crushing noise started initially from the bow area, where the impact had taken place, and I could hear this grinding or groaning of steel, coming ever closer. Bolting out the cabin door toward the ship's port side, away from the noise, I thought that if I could reach the open deck, I might just fling myself over the side and onto whatever awaited me in the dark and fog (including a possible rock). I figured I'd die in the explosion anyway.

Just as I left my cabin, the other ship's hull and bow with which we'd collided sheered away most of the cabin ten feet from me, and water lines were bursting. The water and fog were now rolling into this gaping hole of twisted, mangled steel, grown cherry red from friction. The bathroom and entire chief officer's quarters were gone, but fortunately, the latter was on the ship's bridge.

When I reached the open deck, I could tell the two ships' hulls were locked, and there was no further penetration. Now I hesitated to jump over. The probability of surviving such a jump at night would have been remote. First off, I wouldn't know where I was, and therefore which way to swim; plus the wintertime water of North Florida is very cold, probably in the upper forties. So I looked up toward the port side of the bridge, where I saw some activity, and impulsively ran there to see if I could help in any way.

When I got to the bridge, both the captain and chief officer seemed stunned and bewildered-looking, while the pilot was sitting in a corner weeping. Meanwhile, the helmsman was waiting for someone to give *him* an order. My main concern was all the electrical wiring on board and the fact that there was still power to the circuits, and also that our cargo tanks were obviously ruptured and torn. In other words at any moment we were surely going to have a big explosion, caused by the electrical current coming into contact with the now venting fumes and our cargo spilling into the river!

I remember the captain screaming on the radio for the other ship to "back out, back out!" His purpose was to try to save them from what we all presumed would be an imminent ball of fire. My immediate reaction was to run to the electrical box, where I promptly shut off power in the area where the collision had taken place. The chief officer was not really functional, and between the captain and myself, we exuded, I think, some form of mental coherence. The captain now ordered the chief officer to go aft and organize the crew, getting our lifeboats ready for lowering. As for me, I was told to remain on the bridge and stand by the engines, staying in communication with the engine room.

The other ship's hull meanwhile kept working further and further into us, a little at a time, due to the current; since penetration was so deep, it would obviously be hard for them to back out on the strength of their engines alone. This was, however, right about the time of ebb tide, and as that tide intensified, it allowed the ships to begin disengaging, with the other vessel powering full astern. Some shaky moments took place when the other pilot didn't back out far enough, and the current brought his ship back on us for a near second hit! If you're in the miracle business, here were *two* at one time—and as we all know, you don't ask the Big Guy up there for too many repeats.

Our ship now lay aground on the south shore of the St. John's River, and during the night we inspected it for damage, trying to ascertain how much cargo had leaked out. We determined that at daylight, when the fog had lifted, we would go to the dock, pumping off what cargo we could. As for the rest, we would wash it out of the tanks, then proceed to the shipyard further up river for repairs.

Everyone who came to our battered vessel at the dock, including Gulf Oil's chemists and explosion experts, found themselves completely perplexed as to why these ships, particularly ours, hadn't blown. Based on the types of damage and the kinds of explosive materials we were carrying, plus atmospheric conditions we had encountered, there was no scientific reason for our survival. The best one seemed to come from my wife. As she told me: "I always pray for you and I expect that God's going to protect you."

That brief statement so impacted me that when I came back from the phone, I went directly to the captain's cabin, asking to speak to him for a minute, figuring I'd explain in Susan's pithy manner exactly why our ship hadn't taken the count. He looked quizzical, and with several other guests waiting in his office, he said: "Mate, these gentlemen here will be equally interested in your explanation, since one is an explosion expert, the other a chemist." Partly to introduce me to these men, he added a bit tongue in cheek: "You've received high marks from me for your work, Lance. Go ahead and explain," he smiled. "We're interested."

At that point I asked the experts whether *they* had a theory as to why we had avoided a lethal explosion on our ship. Shaking their heads, they seemed as baffled as the rest of us. I then said that since we couldn't offer any natural, or objectively scientific reasoning for our good fortune, that we ought perhaps to consider my wife's more supernatural explanation, which she had just given me in a single sentence. I then reiterated it to them. They looked over at the captain, and nodding affirmatively, he declared that that was the best damned reason he'd heard for our good fortune, and that we all ought to just take it and run with it!

Chapter 6

Incompetence and Tragedy

AFTER our miraculous deliverance, we arrived at the shipyard, where I immediately received a notice of transfer to another company's ship. There I was to meet one of the most ignorant, insincere, and thoroughly objectionable men I've ever sailed under in my life, Captain Norton De Witt.[4] A New Englander, De Witt had spent forty years on the high seas, but I kid you not that after my first forty *minutes* on the ocean I'd learned more than he had in all those years.

From the outset he and I agreed on nothing. When De Witt came onto the ship's bridge, unlike even the average skipper, his concerns revolved mainly around aesthetics or the cleanliness of the area, instead of other quite significant matters, such as whether the ship was in danger of collision, running onto rocks, etc. There were times when he would talk for hours in a braggadocious manner about what a fine fellow he was—to a captive audience trapped on the bridge. His speeches so nauseated me that I'd walk away right in the middle of these shaggy dog stories, while he continued recounting his exploits. Openly rude, I'd find a wing of the bridge where I was out of earshot, while the other unlicensed crew members were stuck shovelling the BS issuing plentifully from De Witt's mouth.

Unfortunately, my inability to kiss up to such a superior would result inexorably in a bad evaluation, which office staffs without maritime experience might easily take at face value. This was a big problem—that corporate personnel had no ship experience and often didn't know how to read between the lines of reports, or interpret them correctly.

De Witt certainly enjoyed his newly acquired position as master, because he fully expected that everyone around him would follow his own pattern of obsequiousness. Flatterers love to be flattered, and when one failed to do that, he grew angry; little wonder that he increasingly had no use for me. I expected to be judged by the quality of my work and the good attitude I demonstrated re the ship's running,

---

[4]   This is a pseudonym.

TURBULENT SEAS   65

but that was not how De Witt evaluated individuals. Reworking the famed JFK aphorism, he judged people only by what they could do for *him*.

Let me explain what I came to learn about the reason for such bizarre appointments: let's say a ship's skipper has an officer on board who is plainly inept at his jobs, creating a potentially hazardous problem for his superior. If the subaltern has ingratiated himself well enough, and if he happens to be liked by the company's office staff at home, a weak-willed captain may decide to avoid controversy by getting him off the ship via promotion. If that particular captain is looking for further security within the company, this more or less eliminates problems created for him by dangerously bad junior officers. He also gains kudos from the office people for recognizing what they had always suspected—that the character in question is really a good officer, when by objective standards he's not. The smoothie then gets promoted upward, as had obviously happened to De Witt. And the results could become lethal.

It so happened that one of the non-licensed individuals on our vessel, a theoretically able-bodied seaman from Texas named Shane Hardy[5], formed part of my watch. Hardy was responsible for steering the ship at my command eight hours a day. It was common in these watch periods to get into conversations running the gamut from politics to life experiences. Shane was twenty to twenty-five years older than me (in his late forties at the time), but extremely well-built and strong. Eventually he recounted a story about an incident that had occurred in his early twenties, when he'd killed a man with a single blow in a fistfight on the border of Texas and Louisiana—his home area. Apparently he and this other fellow had gotten into their fight after drinking, and with a single blow Shane's punch—from a guy who had been a semi-pro boxer—caused a massive brain haemorrhage in his opponent, and the man died.

Shane explained that this was how he had gotten into the maritime business. The local sheriff was his friend and immediately suggested that Shane vacate the area and join the Merchant Marine, because he didn't want to put up with any more of his problems. Somehow Shane evaded prosecution—having to do with the fact that the victim was from Louisiana and possessed no relatives in the locale where they had tangled.

---

[5]   This is a pseudonym.

Over the years Shane had become very skilled at making nautical items with knots. He could take rope and craft unusual things that were both decoratively tasteful and useful for small boats—dongs on a bell, interesting lanyards, even hammocks. Being adept at and enjoying this hobby so much, Shane generally engaged in it when he was in his cabin and not on duty. Once Captain De Witt became aware of this rope artistry, he thought it wise to make friends with such a man. In fact, he soon started paying Shane out of company funds to make him items from rope for his new sailboat, which De Witt kept in Narragansett Bay up in New England. This created problems for me, as Shane was my subordinate. But it also relieved me of pressures caused whenever De Witt approached during my watch. Now he and Shane spent much time in long conversations, allowing me to move quietly out of the wheelhouse area to a more peaceful bridge.

Shane was a known drinker and in port he often got hammered; but on regaining the ship, he still had to perform cargo watch and other deck responsibilities. On a number of occasions I'd warned him about the gravity of these duties—emphasizing that I expected him to be sober on deck, particularly due to the possibility of contamination of cargo, oil spills, and so on. He seemed to heed these warnings, but let me add that Shane stood about 6'4" and was dauntingly muscular. His biceps were big and he carried very little fat in his body weight. I never felt, however, that because of his size he would stop following my orders. The age difference was a mitigating factor in any potential physical dispute between us. I was tall and young, while Shane was old enough to be my father.

That state of comparative peace ended, however, and with tragic consequences, one night in the port of Tampa. We had a pump man on board named Willie[6], who soaking wet weighed maybe 130 pounds and stood at 5'5" tops. Though sixty-four, Willie was still full of piss and vinegar, an excellent, hard worker, and a family man with seven children at home. You couldn't ask for a more qualified, industrious ship hand, and I spent many hours in his tiny shadow, gleaning tricks of the trade by watching him work. If you showed an interest, he was generous in passing on his considerable maritime knowledge.

During cargo operations in port Willie, along with the ship's officers, would direct seamen like Shane to turn heavy valves and do other bull work. Willie wasn't afraid to break a sweat and perform arduous

---

[6]   This is a pseudonym.

tasks, but there were times when his size hampered him badly, and he needed someone else to help him complete a job.

This particular night in Tampa Shane had switched schedules and was working from four to eight p.m. with the chief officer. Willie was also on deck at the time. By chance I went up there during my off period, ambling over to the gangway to speak with the men working cargo watch. I wanted to learn when the chief officer had determined we would sail and also how cargo operations were going, for in a few hours I'd be on duty and needed insights on what I'd be facing.

As I approached the area where I saw Shane and Willie, I heard a brief, but loud and heated argument taking place. However, I was still some distance away. The chief officer had gone inside for a break, so there was no one else out there. Within a few more steps of noticing the argument unfold, I suddenly saw Shane punch Willie with a powerful uppercut, lifting the older, slighter man right up off his feet and sending him into a back dive onto the steel deck, where he landed head first.

As quickly as the blow was struck, my feet were running full tilt to the scene, starting from about 100 feet away. I had a large head of steam on by the time I reached Shane, ploughing my entire body weight into him, while he still stood over Willie's motionless body. Shane outweighed me by a good fifty pounds, but wasn't prepared to be hit like that. My momentum took him clean off his feet into a section of horizontal pipelines standing two feet off the deck. I now noticed that the assailant reeked strongly of both alcohol and body odor. He'd obviously been on an all-day bender in Tampa. Pinning him into the pipelines, I got one arm around his neck and the other around a pipe, and clasping my hands together, I choked him in order to restrain him. I knew that you didn't give a man like this a second chance. While struggling with Shane in the pipelines, I also hollered for someone to get the chief officer and captain on deck.

It seemed like an eternity before I heard the chief officer approach behind Shane, and I told him to get handcuffs—this man needed restraining. Unfortunately Vic, our chief officer, had a Casper Milquetoast personality, and was generally incapable of rebuking a fly, let alone a human. The whole scene was more than he could bear. He did, however, dash off toward the area of the captain's and officers' cabins, so I presumed he'd do something. By then Shane had pretty much relaxed and I didn't know whether I'd suffocated him, or whether he was simply complying, avoiding any further violence. In any case I didn't let up on him.

A few minutes later Captain De Witt and the chief officer, as well as a couple of deckhands, came out, and immediately the captain ordered me to release his violent friend. Without considering the gravity of the situation—i.e., Willie's life-threatening condition—De Witt simply took Shane up to his cabin, and I didn't see them again for a good thirty minutes.

Meanwhile, Willie was convulsing unconsciously on deck, and the chief officer had gone off to call for an ambulance. I was extremely upset, wanting badly to put Shane in leg irons and restrain him, and to have local authorities make an arrest. I also wanted the captain to validate this process. All these things I wanted—and sadly, I got none of them.

After De Witt had released Shane on his own recognizance, I confronted the captain in his cabin, telling him that it was imperative for civil authorities to take action on this serious matter. I explained to De Witt that Willie was critically injured. The chief officer concurred that the injury was a serious one, and informed us that the ambulance was on its way. But De Witt acted like it was just a sunny day.

The ship's sailing was supposed to be in about four hours, and De Witt's only concern seemed to be that we sail on time. He knew that any introduction here of civil authorities for an investigation would delay our departure, plus call his own competence into question. The chief officer unfortunately wimped out, supporting De Witt, but I was viciously adamant about bringing in relevant authorities. At one point the chief officer grabbed me by the shoulder to restrain me, thinking that I might take a swing at the captain! Which was an exaggeration, though I *was* clearly distraught by the decisions being taken here.

Finally I threw down the gauntlet, and without the usual protocol of calling my superior "Captain," said: "De Witt, if you think you're sailing this ship in four hours without calling in the civil authorities, then you'll sail without the second officer!" I made it clear that sailing without a second officer would violate the law, which placed him between the proverbial rock and hard place. He became lividly angry, responding with a stream of vulgarities, while the chief officer simply stood there in his insipid way, unwilling to back me up. I insisted again that De Witt call in civil authorities, or else I was leaving the ship. Ignoring me, he turned to the chief officer, instructing him to summon the local sheriff. Whereupon I reiterated that the Coast Guard should also be informed of this serious incident. De Witt emphatically repronounced his order to the chief officer—"call the sheriff!"—leaving it at that. No longer able to stand the presence of these two, and without waiting to be told whether I could or could not leave, I departed De Witt's cabin, going back out on deck and waiting anxiously for an ambulance.

The sheriff then arrived, going straight to the captain's cabin, and I was forbidden to speak with him by captain's orders. This allowed De Witt to spin the incident any way he desired, and obviously he wanted to protect a chum who had done so much fancy knot work for him. Meanwhile Shane, released by the captain, had simply disappeared from the ship. But as the sheriff was leaving, I managed to have a brief, private word with him, explaining that I wasn't aware of the content of his conversation with the captain, but that I *was* an eyewitness to the incident. Giving him my name and address, I declared myself available for any court proceeding.

De Witt's ship sailed on time, with his reluctant second officer on board; and in the personal fitness report he filled out for me, he rated me in the worst possible way in virtually every category of my work. He also insisted that once the ship arrived in Texas, I should go on vacation. He didn't have the nerve to fire me. At that point, after hearing of my friend Willie's death, I certainly *needed* a vacation!

A few days later, when I was home in Buffalo, the company called, indicating that it had received De Witt's evaluation (which I hadn't yet seen)—one theoretically requiring my signature. They expressed concern about my ratings, based on the captain's assessment, and said they were going to assign me to a ship bound for the Soviet Union. Gulf Oil vessels rarely departed from U.S. coastlines, but they had recently acquired several grain contracts with the Russians.

The ostensible reason I was reassigned to this upcoming voyage had to do with the fitness report being so poor; but I later found out that it was extremely convenient for Gulf to get me away for a trip of several months abroad, while there were impending legal ramifications stemming from the murder occurring on De Witt's vessel. Apparently the victim's family—his widow and children in Philadelphia—had been contacted by an attorney, and were pursuing legal action to try to provide for a secure future. Being a suddenly destitute widow with seven kids—from teens on down to truly young ones—would be tough for any woman. Willie's widow sought both civil and federal action against the company for the death of her husband. The federal action would be initiated through Coast Guard investigators, and of course the only eyewitness to the event was me. And without an eyewitness account, the whole story could become the fictional version woven by De Witt and any other sycophants who wished to support him.

All this worked out nicely for Shane, a man who in the past had also been able to escape unscathed from the same type of occurrence. After my Russian voyage I would find out that the state of Florida had refused to prosecute or investigate the incident any further than the ten-minute walk on board by the sheriff. They obviously considered it a waste of their tax dollars to spend time on an altercation occurring on a federally registered vessel, even though it was well within their jurisdiction to do so. Since no Floridians were involved (neither victim nor perpetrator), they simply passed up the opportunity to put Shane in a state prison. Willie's widow and her attorney at least hoped that the Coast Guard would prove Shane guilty of *something*, so that in their civil case they might obtain an award or judgment from Gulf Oil. But it was tragic that the Coast Guard lacked my testimony, given that the company had put me out to sea so hastily and on such a long voyage.

The end result—and even this is not certain—was that the family probably received a small settlement from Gulf Oil, though Coast Guard investigators failed to locate sufficient evidence to prosecute Shane for any crime. My only hope was that some day the Just Judge would decide the case.

An ironic footnote to the incident occurred when I was later working for another company, Sabine Transportation. For obviously good reasons Shane had quit Gulf Oil—the company henceforth considering him persona non grata—and then he tried to join one of Sabine's ships on which I was chief officer. As is customary, all non-licensed deck hands had to report to the chief officer when they joined a ship. After hearing a knock at my door, I nearly fell out of my chair to see this violent thug enter the office. My emotions were mixed and bewildered. I didn't know if I should jump up and hit Shane or not. I was simply numb to see this animal standing there before me, but somehow managed to ask him what he wanted. He said he had just joined the company and that they had assigned him to this ship. I responded that I did indeed have an opening for an able seaman.

"But I can tell you this," I added emphatically, "that it'll be a cold day in hell before you'll ever sail with me again!" I then told him to get his gear and posterior off the ship—immediately. I also told him that I hoped he had a dime to call up our office, so that he could inform them why he wasn't joining the vessel. Because *I'd* be telling them so within the hour. And that's the last I ever saw of Shane. He slunk away, kind of meekly, hopefully feeling some guilt or shame. And in an odd way I felt a momentary twinge of pity for him too, though not nearly as much as I felt for Willie's widow and children. This unexpected meeting had stirred up painful memories—of a good man who had taught me a lot, and whose existence had ended prematurely. But on ships or off, I guess this life guarantees us nothing....

Chapter 7

To Russia with Vodka

TO recapitulate, De Witt's distorted fitness report had come out, then the company reassigned me to another vessel, a big one of 38,000 deadweight tons. Gulf Oil had four ships built to this size, their largest class of U.S. flagship. I joined the vessel in late April, 1976, and we started cleaning her up—"gas-freeing" the ship and preparing to load corn and grain for transport to Odessa, Russia.

After several days' work the ship passed inspection by U.S. Food and Drug Administration inspectors, who certified it clean enough for us to carry the grain. So we proceeded to Baltimore, under a skipper who was De Witt's antithesis—easy-going, but also somewhat of a black sheep in the sense that he hadn't known how to butter up company staffers. This fellow was far from Gulf's most admired sea captains, but at least ship's officers found him easy to work with. He was simply incapable of making the political moves necessary to elicit warm office support and therefore, had no special perks with the home base.

Our chief officer was a young man about three years older than me, a graduate of Maine Maritime, located in Castine, Maine. This Jack Casey[7] was a heavy drinker and I was surprised, given his age, that he had already become such a serious alcoholic. Three-quarters baked most of the time, he was, as you might expect, divorced, and also quite a womanizer. In every port if he wasn't drunk, he was with a woman. If he was drunk, he was still frequently with a woman. And when he wasn't with a woman, he was *looking* for one.

The other officer was our young third mate, a graduate of Texas Maritime named Neil Lord.[8] But we referred to him as Lord Lollipop, because he was a skinny little runt afraid of his own shadow, and always seemed to be on the verge of tears. He never seemed to have had enough rest to satisfy him and he was very anti-social. Whenever he was offered overtime work, he categorically refused, preferring to remain horizontal as much as possible. Even in a vertical position Neil

---

[7]   This is a pseudonym.
[8]   This is a pseudonym.

never seemed to reveal much common sense, and whenever I, his superior, had work details with him, I was invariably disappointed by his general lack of interest, his inveterate laziness, and really, just the strange way about him.

Meanwhile, as dysfunctional as Jack, our chief officer, was due to his drinking bouts, at least during his sober periods I could get along with him. We would laugh and joke about different life situations we'd encountered, and during these sober times it was always fun to talk to Jack. But when he drank, he would get downright mean. Even in those drunk periods he never physically challenged me, but at the drop of a hat he would terrorize most anyone else. Experienced crew members understood his personality type well, and usually kept a discreet distance. But of course those with a lust for booze chummed up to him, and so Casey got along well with all the shipboard drinkers. Any unlicensed sailors predisposed to imbibing had a staunch friend in Chief Officer Jack, for they shared a common problem.

I suppose I had relaxed a bit, because I just wasn't too concerned about all this. On that voyage to Russia I didn't allow myself to care too much about anything, for the previous one had left such a bad taste in my mouth. This time around I decided to distance myself from day-to-day personnel problems on board, simply tending to my own duties.

I did, however, become chummy with the second assistant engineer, who stood watch in the engine room at times when I was on the bridge. Appropriately enough, his name was Dave Coffin. Dave became far and away my closest friend on board, and between him, myself, and the chief officer we managed to create a fairly workable, three-way camaraderie. When Dave was off watch, so was I, so we would pal around a bit, discussing different things or maybe playing some cribbage. I had previously sailed with this only child, whose father and mother were successful dentists in the Portland, Maine area. On previous voyages, whenever we arrived at the latter port, Dave's parents would invariably prepare a huge New England lobster feast for their son and any of his friends who could get off watch to visit their fine beachside home.

On the present voyage Dave was excited by the fact that having been many years without a girlfriend, he'd gotten engaged prior to sailing—to a young lady he felt would make him a good wife. In his leisure time Dave's principal conversational focus was on this soon-to-be bride, plus his investments and a new home he had just built. Sadly he would never get to enjoy any of these things, because inside of a year he would be fatally electrocuted while sailing for the first time as a chief engineer. Dave was truly a good friend of mine, and when I later heard about his death while I myself was at sea, it was very painful. At the time of his death he was only weeks away from marriage. He had been working by himself on a problem with the ship's steering engine motor, apparently without assistance; and then he was found electrocuted. A good man and an excellent engineer was lost in the process.

To regain the thread, when our Russian-bound ship was in the port of Baltimore, the stevedores loaded cargo in daylight hours only. So part of our evenings was usually spent shooting rats on the pier with a gas-powered pellet gun we had purchased. Animal lovers shouldn't recoil in horror, for some of these rats were so big and hardy that the pellets simply bounced off them, and they probably suffered no more than they would have from, say, flea bites. But Lord Lollipop never endorsed this type of entertainment, convinced that the death of any animal at human hands was vicious and sadistic.

After about a week's loading we departed, heading across the Atlantic for Gibraltar. Basically the weather was fair in this late springtime. We made landfall on the coast of Morocco, then navigated along the northern coast of Africa through the Dardanelles and Bosporus Strait into the Black Sea, arriving in the city of Odessa about late May or early June 1976.

It was both interesting and somewhat weird to find myself behind the Iron Curtain for the first time, and to witness the stark drabness of Odessa. First off, came the Russian people's clothing—with little or no color. Everything here just seemed to have a brown, sandstone kind of sameness to it. In that country there was evidently no need for color, for there was no private industry which alone puts a premium on liveliness in a society. There were no advertising signs whatsoever. In fact there was little that would cause a human being to turn his head and have a second look. People here were simply non-descript. Some Russians did, however, wear blue jeans, highly sought after as a black market commodity. They paid exorbitant amounts for these articles of western clothing, or even for things like chewing gum, which they always called "Chiclets." "Have you got any Chiclets?" was the cry we would frequently hear in Russia. The black market truly flourished here.

Prior to departing Baltimore, our chief officer had made sure to buy himself a cache of make-up compacts and pantyhose, which he could then use judiciously in the Soviet Union to secure goodly amounts of female company and vodka. Casey had also made the astute purchase of several gallons of grain alcohol, legal in some states (including Maryland)—a clear-looking liquid which is obviously very dangerous to the human body. At first I figured Jack had stashed this liquid on board for his own consumption, but later learned that he would use it to help him outdo Russian longshoremen in drinking contests.

On our arrival in Odessa the 1976 Summer Olympics were starting up, and Russian stevedore bosses would report to us each day on how many Soviets had won events, beating their chests with great pride. When Americans won events, it was never discussed. In this competitive atmosphere Jack, our patriotic chief officer, decided it was time to take up the stevedores' challenge—i.e., that the Russians could outdrink any American on the ship. So taking out the grain alcohol he had brought, he carefully spiked several bottles of vodka. All the bottles still looked identical and clear, but Jack knew which ones were spiked. Carefully pouring the Russians his loaded versions of Stolichnaya, Jack made it his nightly routine to challenge any and all Soviet stevedores on the ship to a truly Olympian drinking contest.

Each morning I was amazed to find Jack not only still alive, but functioning more or less like the rest of us—partially helped by his body size; while there were generally three or four semi-conscious Russians lying inert in passageways. Jack knew how embarrassing this was to them. When a Russian passed out in his cabin at some point during the night, he'd simply have the man dragged out into the passageway for public display and humiliation. The next day their wives came looking for these besotted spouses. Since they weren't allowed to go on board, the women simply waited on the dock, screaming at other Russian longshoremen who were busy working, trying to find out their inebriated husbands' whereabouts. This nightly and daily routine went on for several weeks, and I'm sure there were a number of liver transplants—if those then existed in Russia—as a result.

In the mornings I was frequently given the duty of lugging these comatose creatures down to the gangway. Once they arrived on the dock, their irate wives would then kick, punch, and berate them, dragging them home by their ears. We Americans watched all this with a broad smile on our faces. Cold War booze contests...

Despite its drabness, Odessa was an important Black Sea resort area for the entire Ukraine and Soviet Union—its summertime beaches littered with Communist Party officials. Their *dachas* were located in this region, though generally secluded from the actual beach playgrounds. But even the Communist elite was always deprived of and desperately in search of western clothing; anything that made them appear more powerful than the next person would be highly sought after. Officials who could acquire things like that on the black market were considered formidable men, and the average Russian feared them greatly. Yet whenever these Soviet bigwigs gathered together on some public occasion in my presence, they always trumpeted the Party Line—to the effect that socialism was the higher moral road, while western capitalism encouraged greed and self-exaltation! Americans also placed huge burdens on their poor, causing our society to become polarized between haves and have nots. That was the public line we generally heard.

But in private conversations Soviet hypocrisy would invariably rear its crimson head. Communist officials actively set up private conferences with me in order to negotiate, always trying to exchange their worthless junk for something offered up by our evil capitalist system, obviously worth much more to them. Most commonly they tried to sell us Russian army clothing, especially belts bearing a red sickle and hammer, items that many Americans desired for souvenirs. Frankly I could care less about such things. To me the insignias on those belts merited no accolades, and I didn't want to hang them around my house. I recall bringing home a few such belt buckles for friends and neighbors, symbolic to me of an oppressed society and of a people who would have loved to have a happier, more fruitful existence, and more personal freedom.

In sum, these one-on-one sessions with Russian dignitaries were comical to me, and I never failed to mention their duplicitous ways. Frequently I would bait them on purpose, asking why they would be interested in anything having to do with the West, when publicly they denigrated us. This threw them into consternation, because these supposedly dedicated Communists obviously worshipped us, envying everything we produced and stood for. Maybe they were just confused. To some degree they appeared to believe Soviet propaganda and lies; yet before their eyes they saw the fruits of capitalism lusciously dangling, driving their basic human cravings to higher and higher levels. Aware of this mindset, I could use such knowledge to my advantage in the future, particularly on a second voyage to Russia in 1979, by which time I knew how to exploit their weaknesses and ideological inconsistencies to get shipboard jobs done more efficiently.

But I really need to describe further the deep gloom that pervaded Odessa, which at the time was more than just physical, but something in the disposition of the people. When you saw women lined up 50 to

150 deep, waiting for a shop to open in the morning because there was such a shortage of whatever item that shop specialized in; and then witnessed them pushing and shoving each other, having already stood in line as much as five and six hours during the night, it became truly depressing. Workers responsible for opening the shop might or might not arrive on time—carelessness about jobs and time itself was endemic to Communist Russia in its last era. Almost every female I beheld in Russia carried a mesh bag at the ready, and it was not unusual to walk down the street and see a riot break out, when suddenly women would rush madly toward a shop about to open, having heard a report that *something* might be available, i.e., that was not normally obtainable. (Which meant virtually everything!) The only item that didn't seem to be in dire shortage was bread. This was one of the few food staples I loved in Russia—black bread in heavy, dense, round loaves, one of them almost a meal in itself. But shortages of vegetables, meat, fruit, and the rest were beyond American belief.

The streets of Odessa were almost entirely made of cobblestone, and it was extremely rare to see asphalt pavement. You would see old women with their assigned duties as street sweepers standing around with brooms—sticks bundled together at the end of a larger stick. The contraption was more of a long pole than a broom. Of course such things weren't manufactured professionally here; these were simply pieces of wood that had fallen from the trees and which the old women then bundled up. At least Odessa's streets were clean, and I never saw much of a problem with crime there. The low crime rate was a big issue for the Soviets to brag about, but what they failed to add was that they had no freedom either.

Most women you'd see cleaning streets were elderly, disfigured, hunched-over grandmas, who by all appearances had lived very hard lives. Occasionally you would notice a younger woman doing this job, but not often. Later I learned that if this were the case, it was only because that woman had committed some terrible crime against Soviet society, causing her to lose her regular job. Like the mythical Russian *balaïaga* who sweeps for an eternity behind her, these women would be condemned to a lifetime of menial work.

In my peregrinations around Odessa I don't recall ever seeing fresh paint anywhere. As noted, there was little variation in color, and nothing that was very attractive. By western standards architecture and construction of buildings in the old city was pathetic. Whenever an old edifice fell down, the Soviets would simply re-chink the stone from the antiquated structure, using it to construct a new one, and they did so over a long period, because there was no impetus to get anything done on time. Whether you worked or didn't work, you made the same amount.

Corruption seemed ubiquitous in the former Soviet Union. As an example, I learned through my womanizing chief officer that a new-found female friend of his was employed as a nurse at the local hospital, but made so much money hustling foreign sailors that she could pay off her boss in sought-after western currency; consequently, she never had to show up for work at the hospital. In many cases their bosses simply became pimps controlling these so-called nurses. Medical backgrounds benefited Russian prostitutes, affording them easy access to a limited supply of antibiotics so needed in their trade.

Besides these Soviet oddities, we had some of our own on board ship. One could start with Lord Lollipop, our third officer, who, as noted, had a very meek demeanor, and was quickly picked on by the hardened Russian stevedores. During his cargo watches Neil was timid giving instructions, and whenever he was out on deck, they would double over with laughter most of the time. This frustrated the chief officer more than it did me, because Casey had complete responsibility for efficient discharge of cargo. Some discord developed between the chief and his third officer, and I was amused, watching their tussles from the sidelines. I remember one day when the chief officer asked his subaltern not to go ashore because he needed additional work done on the ship, and Lord Lollipop moaned that he wanted badly to go into town, because he had an important appointment.

The chief raised his eyebrows, remarking sardonically to his wet-behind-the-ears third: "So—you met yourself a Russian honey?"

"No," replied Neil. "I just want to take pictures of some of the Russian buildings and monuments for my mother." Casey looked at him in disbelief, answering in a very straightforward manner: "Forget going ashore today. If you want pictures to bring home, you can get them another time." Here was Neil all saddled up with his camera and ready to take pictures of an alien world before him, and now he looked crestfallen. So Jack relented a bit, noting that he himself was going ashore on some business and that he would be very glad to take pictures for his downcast third officer. If Neil gave him the camera, why he would take some really neat snapshots of buildings and of the Russian community here.

Pondering, and finding it hard to trust, Lord Lollipop nonetheless agreed. "I'll stay here," he said, "but you get me some good pictures!" And the chief officer said, "Oh yeah, don't you worry. Your mother will *love* them." With that Neil changed clothes to go back on deck to work, and Jack looked at me with a nasty smile. "Boy, will I get his mother some shots!" he declared. Snatching the camera off the desk, Casey ran ashore in his street clothes, and as I looked over the rail, I saw him already embracing his new girlfriend and heading down the dock.

Many hours later, at about two in the morning, and while I was still working, Jack returned, his clothing dishevelled, and his body reeking of its usual back-to-ship odor, that is, the smell of liberal doses of alcohol. He had scuff marks and dirt on his nice street clothes, but with a big smile asked me to come up to the officers' cargo office. There he took the camera, dropped it on the counter, and tapping it with his finger, said: "Do you want to know what kind of pictures I got for Neil's mom?" I said I didn't think so. He said: "I'm gonna tell you anyway, Lance." He then gave me a frame-by-frame description of every seedy prostitute working in Odessa. He even told me that he'd had a few pictures left on the roll, which he then took of pigeons copulating in the square near the famous war memorial monument there. In two hours Casey was scheduled to go on watch, and both he and I knew that if he lay down for a while, I would end up working his watch too, because he'd never get up. So I sat there trying to hold his attention, having no desire, unless ordered, to take over for him. For two hours I pumped him with coffee, while he discussed his escapades of the day, laying on the detail. I would often think about Neil getting up the next morning, very excited and gratified that the chief officer had taken time to visit all the different monuments and photograph them for him. Why he had even gone to the opera house to take pictures of the ladies singing there (so Casey told him). Jack also suggested that Neil write down a picture log and include that in the missive to his mother. Neil was apparently so thrilled that with unusual alacrity, he got the film packaged up and put into the mail, wanting it to reach the U.S. as soon as possible. During long sea watches for years afterward, I would often try to imagine the expression that came across his mother's face on seeing her son's pictures of Odessa's sights!

On most ships sick people prone to deranged behavior were easy enough to find—from the top echelons to the bottom. But Casey's colorful character was one of a kind, and never ceased to amaze me. Well liked by Gulf's office staff back home, both because he was a hard worker and a voluble fellow, he now had to spread his human magic here in the land of Communist boozehounds. For the longshore bosses on the ship had arranged a special dinner to honor our captain and officers at the famed Krasny Hotel[1] in Odessa (Krasny meaning red). To the average Russian that hotel was the crème de la crème, the Pierre or Crillon of their city.

On arrival it did reveal more color inside than was normal, since the hotel was designed only for elite Russians in the Party and for western visitors traveling here. They even had the finest of Russian toilet paper on hand—in some instances yesterday's newspaper, but in the more expensive suites, real stuff with the consistency of wax paper. Moving to the food they served, a pampered American might be a little disappointed, particularly if he or she ordered meat. Even at this chic hotel the steak they served was at best suited for the palate of a dog. It was gristly as a cactus, and basically inedible. The most common meat available was sausage, but God knows what animal parts were in this stuff!

In addition to such drawbacks in a supposedly "luxury" establishment, the hotel's standards of cleanliness were low as well. I would find that even in the finest Russian restaurants everything was filthy, and you took your life in your hands eating there. You would never, ever consider drinking the water, and I should also point out that it was normal in a city of 10 million or so to see outhouses behind apartment buildings, because those buildings lacked plumbing. Honey dippers with horse-drawn wagons were a common sight on these cobblestone streets—people whose job was to scoop the excrement from these outhouses. They would lower buckets down there and then by hand, dump the waste into huge vats on the back of the wagons. I didn't spend much time observing that appetite-defeating operation, though perhaps Neil got a picture of it for his mother.

When we entered the Krasny's dining room, first appearances deceived, since each table bore white linen with fine silver and crystal goblets. Like something out of Gogol's *Dead Souls* the linen was a bit yellowed, the silver tarnished, but the crystal—crucial to one of Casey's most amazing feats soon to be performed—was nice and clear.

As the evening wore on, more and more vodka was consumed, along with an absolutely vile Russian wine. Since I avoided drinking any of the water, the only beverage I could sample was a small amount of that wine. Even then I prayed that the alcohol had murdered any critters that might be lurking in the glass. As a disinfectant this libation might do the job, but it sure tasted awful.

---

[1] Sometimes called the Krasnàyà Hotel (feminie of adjective).

As festivities progressed, Casey and our captain grew ever more drunk, along with the mayor of Odessa and other Soviet authorities, for this was a significant event with a significant goal: to establish good relations with visiting Americans who might satisfy that insatiable Communist appetite for black market items. You couldn't go to the bathroom alone, for one of these officials would try to converse with you—i.e., to find out whether you had any jeans, chewing gum, books, anything at all, which they would then buy. Of course their rubles were worthless, and in fact would have been more useful as toilet paper, being softer in texture than what they had on hand.

With alcohol consumption crescendoing to some dizzy pinnacle of inebriation around the Krasny dining room, louder and louder conversations were heard, on the subject of who could outdo whom in the fine art of guzzling. Some Russians at the party obviously felt they were prepared to try and outdrink this now famous chief officer, and poor Casey knew he couldn't spike the vodka here, as he had done on the ship. So it was time to pull out another rabbit from his truly versatile bag of tricks.

Without any warning he suddenly stood up, offering a grandiose toast to the mayor of Odessa and his many pals, including the police chief and every notable Communist figure for miles around, including the longshore bosses. It was a long, shaggy dog toast near the party's close. The longshore bosses, who had invited us here, were still a little gun shy of any alcoholic challenge the redoubtable Casey might offer. They had been beaten soundly by their wives, and figured the American could simply out-swill any comer. In profuse, glowing words Jack continued to acknowledge the party officials, using an interpreter to convey his message; and finally, he raised his glass for the toast, slugged down the vodka, and then held the empty glass to show all the bosses. He now solemnly intoned: "Everyone join me in this special occasion," and promptly bit a chunk out of the glass, chewed it, and sat down! People in the place were shocked, and utterly silent. I thought I could hear the mice's little feet pattering beneath the tables, and almost their conversations. Everyone watched Casey, as he now proceeded to chew up the glass made of fine Russian crystal, and as it somehow slid down his palate. Over the next fifteen minutes we all remained awestruck and in dumbfounded silence, as Jack carefully chewed and consumed that entire glass from the base through the stem to the open goblet. In my life I'd never seen anything quite like this exploit, and I was as flabbergasted as everyone else here. I knew for sure that no one in the room could follow or top such an act. And I thought that by morning I'd be promoted to chief officer, because Casey would surely be dead!

After swallowing the glass's last shards, he gawked with a broad smile at every face in the place. Searching for appropriate words, Odessa's mayor now offered a toast, his eyes still bulging, and fully expecting to see Casey fall over dead at any moment! After offering his toast, he dismissed his party minions and broke up the party. Our private car and driver waiting at the front of the hotel took us back to the ship, and for a while I wasn't sure what to say to Casey about what he had just done. I think the first thing I finally asked him was whether he had a steel sphincter, because I sure hoped that when that glass came out the next day—*if* it came out—that it would do so easier than it had gone down. I truly wondered how Casey would digest it, and what would happen to his body.

I'm sure he could perceive my obvious befuddlement, so he tried to soothe me with his response, telling me: "Lance, I've done this since my college days. You just have to chew the glass very carefully and everything will work out."

The next day Casey seemed to be functioning normally, but for several days afterward, I still expected to see him drop dead at any time. For weeks we intermittently discussed his appetite for crystal. Each day the Russian longshoremen came on board, asking whether this human phenomenon was OK, obviously expecting to learn that he had passed away. They remained utterly cowed for the remainder of our time there. The Summer Olympics were at their peak and as noted earlier, the Russians would still give us a daily report of their victories. But this was probably the most amazing Olympic event any of us had ever seen, and it was an American victory.

July 4 was rapidly approaching, and for about a week prior to it the chief officer sent out word to those who had attended the celebration at the Krasny, announcing that he was going to host a Bicentennial birthday party on the beach in celebration of America's independence. Of course as the party's host Casey got to provide a number of things, including the beverages. By this time our captain had quietly distanced himself from the chief officer and the rest of the crew. In fact I didn't see too much of him. He spent a lot of time in his cabin reading, or perhaps figuring out how to treat someone for glass poisoning!

Since the wine tasted so poorly in Russia, Casey decided he'd make an instant batch of his own, transporting it in our large coffee urns to the beach. The chief took every drop of the ship's grape juice, mixing it with grain alcohol, and somehow produced something more savorous than the Russian brand we'd drunk at the Krasny. The weather for the Fourth turned out to be perfect. It was exceptionally warm for the Black Sea area, bright and sunny, and in the high 70s or low 80s. The sea water was always very cold and salty here, and in fact this was a poor excuse for a beach, though to the Russians it was a top-of-the-line resort.

Casey also brought a newly invented cassette player to provide background music for the party. Even to Americans this kind of boom box was still a desirable, novel device, and Casey had purchased a large one, which he'd already used for the Olympic drinking bouts he had hosted on board ship. Transporting the machine to the beach, we filled it with Decel flashlight-type batteries for power. The only song we played at the party on an almost continuous basis was the Beatles "Back in the U.S.S.R," enjoyed by all.

Casey was his usual gregarious self, inviting many of the local hospital nurses to the bash, some of whom quickly tried to cozy up to me. But I offered no encouragement, telling Jack's English-speaking consort to convey to these women that they should keep their distance, and their hands off me—I was a married man. But I did end up enjoying the day. Many local Party officials came by, and at one point early in the celebration a policeman approached, trying to quell the noise from the boom box and some of the revelry going on, until he recognized these Communist notables lifting their glasses. Before his quick retreat, the cop extended profuse, self-abasing apologies to these regional mafiosi.

As the day lengthened and the Russians grew ever more inebriated, they really got into the celebration of America's Bicentennial, singing "Back in the U.S.S.R." in English, by now permanently engraved inside everyone's skull. I know I will never forget this celebration. While other tall ships rested in New York's harbor, many thousands of sea miles away, on the beaches of Odessa we celebrated with them, and even the Russians felt themselves a part of it. Was this some kind of precursor of the upcoming Soviet collapse under Gorbachev?

Shortly after the Bicentennial celebration, we departed the Soviet Union, sailing westward back home. I had, however, made several acquaintances during this stay of almost two months, standing me in good stead for the future. I now knew how Russian stevedore bosses operated—their Soviet tactics of intimidation having become familiar ground under my feet. I understood something of the country's social fabric and its power structure. I saw how Communists would bully Americans, manipulating them into tight jams, in order to blackmail them into handing over western goodies. All this represented invaluable local knowledge for my next voyage to Russia several years later, my first as a captain of America's largest ship ever built to that date. As the Beatles sang about Stalin always being on "mi-mi-mi-mi mind," maybe it should, in fact, have been "Jack Jack Jack...."

Chapter 8

Back to American Scalawags

ABOUT a year later and early in my employment with Apex Marine, I was assigned as chief officer during the summer of 1977 to a coast-wise ship called the *S.S. Virgo*, a jumbo-sized T-2 tanker. Originally constructed late in World War II, its mid-body was subsequently expanded to a point where it had increased carrying capacity by approximately 40%. The captain assigned to the vessel was a wartime graduate of the Maritime Academy at King's Point, an older gentleman with whom I immediately felt a father-son relationship developing. Quite unlike my own father, however, this captain had a serious problem with alcohol, about as constant in our trade as on the pages of Hemingway or Fitzgerald. The man was so physically drained from his frequent drinking bouts that he could offer little real assistance in the performance of my duties as chief officer. I soon realized that the company's assignments to the vessel had been made to put the strong in with the weak, me being the strong and he being a kindly old gentleman, a worn-out sea dog, to put it most charitably.

Even though I carried the real command load here, it wasn't by legal authority—it was *de facto* rather than *de jure*. A chief officer *can* do a lot, but he always answers to the captain, that is, if the captain is there. And by that I mean mentally! Our Captain Bob[9] would frequently be on vacation in some other land of the mind, locked in his cabin drinking himself silly, lost to the rest of us and getting so corked that he often ended up urinating all over himself, then lying in a pool of his own making. There were frequent occasions when Captain Bob was conspicuously missing for several days, and the only way I knew he was still on board was because of noxious odors seeping out the door-vent slats from his cabin and office.

Checking on him daily, it was quite normal for me to find this odd fellow bombed in his bunk. I would then gather up his empty bottles, tossing them overboard (recycling not yet in vogue). Our Captain Bob was a Scotch drinker—the brand or grade made no difference; but if there was no Scotch or other liquor on board, he'd drink anything

---

[9]   This is a pseudonym.

containing alcohol, including aftershave lotion and Listerine (the latter one of his favorites, with its yellow hue somewhat resembling his beloved Scotch). When we tried to purchase mouthwash from the ship's store, we would sometimes find all the Listerine stock gone.

One should also mention that during frequent drunken stints Captain Bob neither bathed nor shaved. So it was sadly comical when he laboriously got himself together in a sobering-up period, especially the first few hours, when he'd arrive at the officers' ward room or the galley area, sitting down to eat with us in teeshirt and khaki trousers, reeking of booze and urine. His Bluto-type beard, usually five or six days old, carried in it some carpet lint, to which he would generally add bits of scrambled eggs, grits, and toast crumbs, before staggering back to his cabin to clean up further.

The moment Captain Bob poked his head into the ward room, it was like a Chinese fire drill for the officers, running for the back door. Sadly, he was a laughingstock to all of us. But during his sober periods, the man turned out to be extremely intelligent, shockingly so. It was amazing that he had any brain cells at all, because they were so sautéd in booze I was surprised they still functioned. Captain Bob loved cribbage and especially crossword puzzles, and spent many hours working at the latter in his cabin. Anyone wishing to gain his favor during these sober periods needed only to hand him a puzzle, or preferably, a book of them, and he was instantly on your side. I should add that during his drunken times he never acknowledged my assistance, for he was in complete denial about his problem. But somehow I felt sorry for him, as he did have a fine mind.

His personal life? As one might expect, Captain Bob's resumé was littered with several divorces and kids from different marriages, who probably grew up as rebellious detriments to society. The captain was of course divorced at the time I knew him, remaining so until he died.

The entire ship was aware that I called virtually all the shots here, putting me in a position where those jealous of authority could feel I was something of a usurper. This created friction with certain individuals beneath me in the chain of command. One should also understand that each time the ship docked at a continental U.S. port, there would be a turnover of some portion of the crew, either through vacations, employment termination, or death, though the latter was rarer.

In Charleston, S.C. two apparently able-bodied seamen joined our vessel, assigned duties within my jurisdiction in the deck department. Shortly after they boarded the ship and we were back out at sea, I discovered that they too had a drinking problem. These guys were good friends—both in their mid-twenties or so, maybe a year younger than me. Because of the age similarity they at first assumed, I think, that I would find them interesting characters, and perhaps felt they had located another potential drinking buddy. In fact, the gulf between us was wider than either understood, due to the fact that my position was tantamount to captain. Even as chief officer, the gap between my rank and theirs would have been a great one. In other words conversations for the most part would be one-way—from me to them....

Early one morning I was called by the second officer and informed that neither of these two new deckhands had reported for duty; so I visited their cabin, where I found them trashed in their bunks—i.e., dead drunk. I woke them up, telling them curtly that they had fifteen minutes to report to my office, and that they should come dressed for work.

On their arrival I read them the riot act, explaining that any further behavior of this sort would result in immediate dismissal. If the situation warranted it, I would have the captain log them, which meant putting into the official record problems they presented on American vessels. Being logged resulted in a hearing conducted by the U.S. Coast Guard and sometimes in severe punishment, including prison terms, fines, suspensions, or revocation of a seaman's license. What these characters didn't know was that our captain was never in any condition to conduct an examination of evidence, in order to determine whether they should be logged in the first place! And only the captain could institute an official log entry. So my authority was badly hampered because of Captain Bob's frequently incapacitated condition. Though most of the crew, including these two individuals, were unaware of it, I was really in a powerless disciplinary position. The whole thing became somewhat of a strategic game for me, because I never knew when the captain would be sober enough that I could even notify him of the type of events going on, and it was always important to act quickly when it came to disciplinary action. By law, loggings had to be officially entered in the book within twenty-four hours of an actual incident, and given Captain Bob's extended periods of other-worldliness, it was almost impossible to have this weapon to brandish.

The two deckhands sheepishly apologized for not having turned out on time, and I warned them again that any further dereliction of duty would be dealt with severely. The ship was en route to St. Croix in the U.S. Virgin Islands, about sixty miles south of St. Thomas, where we frequently loaded at the Hess Oil Refinery on the island's south side. For the remaining several days of the voyage these two individuals worked hard, and were essentially model citizens; however, they knew they were under watchful scrutiny on my part, and I made no bones about their probationary status. Many times when they were working on deck under an immediate superior, I just happened to walk by, acknowledging their presence. But nothing further... In hindsight I think this may have frustrated them, because they probably hoped I'd stop to converse with them, establishing some sort of relationship. My focus, however, was not on social matters, but on work issues and performance of the vessel. The *Virgo* carried very dangerous cargo, including highly volatile gasolines and other toxic chemicals, and there was simply no latitude for me to socialize, especially since I had the captain's administrative duties to carry out, as well as my own.

The two pals were assigned directly to duties under a second officer, standing watch from twelve noon to four p.m. on the ship's bridge. They also stood watch from midnight to four a.m, which filled out their eight-hour work day. During morning hours they frequently worked overtime at various tasks. While on bridge watch, it was their duty to steer the ship, maintaining a vigilant lookout for other vessels and potential hazards.

The ship arrived in St. Croix, and our stay there went off without a hitch, except that just as we were about to pull away, we noticed these two fellows were not on board (it had been about a thirty-six hour layover, loading a volatile assortment of hydrocarbons, gasolines, heating oils, jet fuels, petrochemicals, and the like). While we were literally casting off lines, a taxicab came racing down the pier, with these two derelicts jumping out of the still-moving vehicle, screaming frantically for us to wait! I kept the gangway from being raised for an additional thirty seconds, giving them just enough time to scramble on board. Then I told them to drop the boxes and cartons they were carrying and to report immediately to the second officer on the ship's stern, busy taking up mooring lines with a short-staffed crew (because of their absence). One of the latecomers indicated he wished to change into work clothes and I told him he should have thought about that by being here on time. So he had to run aft with shiny street shoes on, soon to be ruined by salt water and slop that would run off the mooring lines as he brought them up on board. But I had little compassion for those who didn't pull their weight here on a consistent basis. It was also frustrating to watch the captain neglect to pull *his* weight, but for some reason I liked the guy, given that he had something special about him. Whereas for these fellows I had zero tolerance.

The ship was now heavily laden, and we then ran northward to the Virginia Capes, discharging cargo in several ports of the Tidewater area, and finally ending up at the last port of Philadelphia. The ship was then scheduled to return to St. Croix for reloading. That return voyage would be full of hard work, since we had major cargo changes coming up, and the cargo tanks had to be prepared to prevent contaminations of the new load. Based on the character of the upcoming cargo to be carried, it was my duty to calculate mathematically various weights and to place materials throughout the vessel in the right way, so as not to strain the ship's capacity. This entailed a lot of labor, especially with all the washing and ventilation required to avoid contamination.

By now it was apparent that these two guys had party-boy mentalities while in port, but when impelled in the right direction, could demonstrate a relatively hard-working mentality at sea; that is, once sobered up sufficiently from their shoreside stints. In many cases alcoholics feel that's reason enough to get by in life—that really, they are OK as is. Many in our occupation felt that once they got out to sea and could sober up and work hard, that they would somehow locate the good graces of their supervising officers. I never fell into this manipulative trap drunks liked to set for their superiors, because I always knew by experience that boozers were hazardous to ships dealing constantly with dangerous materials and potentially perilous situations.

Once we reached St. Croix again, these two fellows decided to stock up on their alcoholic reserves, as liquor down there was cheaper than soft drinks. Hence, in defiance of maritime law, and unbeknownst to me, they bought numerous cases of liquor, secretly loading them onto the ship while I was sleeping. They stored the cases down in the ship's bowels, and in an area seldom used. They even painted the boxes, so that the J&B Scotch labels on the outside of the cartons were camouflaged.

But leaving St. Croix on this return trip, they failed to sober up, so I decided then and there to terminate their employment. Once we were a day out at sea and their heads had sufficiently cleared, I called them to my office, and with a second officer as witness, I fired both men, informing them that when we reached our first port of call, Jacksonville, Florida, they were to depart the vessel. The two men argued in the presence of the second officer that I was a heartless, insensitive taskmaster, and that they had worked very hard for me, and I should take that into consideration. I'm sure that my ensuing lecture thoroughly angered them, as I discussed the importance of their responsibilities and the great dangers always present in the operation of this vessel. I concluded by declaring that we really didn't need such types working on our tanker; and that if it were up to me, and not against the law, I'd simply cut them adrift in a boat! I also reminded them that they must still perform their remaining duties as required by law, meaning that they should stand watches in a prudent, responsible manner, following all commands the second officer gave them. I asked if they had any questions regarding their duties and responsibilities, but neither did.

That scene had occurred during the day, and the following morning at four a.m., as was my custom, I went out to the ship's bridge. My times for standing watch were from four to eight in the morning and also from four to eight p.m. At four a.m. and four p.m. I relieved the second officer of his bridge duties. In other words my routine was well known to the off-going watch, including these two liquor-loving individuals. The moment I set foot on the bridge in the early morning hours—it was always dark—I gravitated toward the pot of coffee, freshly brewed as a courtesy to the incoming watch. This coffee was for officers only, but unlicensed deckhands had to prepare it.

Groping through the darkness of the bridge that bleary morning, I got over to the pot, and by instinct knew the location of my cup. I grabbed the handle of the hot pot, pouring in a very dim light what I presumed to be a cup of coffee. As usual I began discussing with the second officer what had transpired on his watch during the night concerning navigation and other shipboard matters. For some reason I didn't bring the coffee cup directly to my lips, as there must have been some discussion taking my attention away from it. I stepped back into the chart room, an area behind the bridge in the heart of the ship's navigation area, and in somewhat better light examined the chart to ascertain our position. I would never take control of the vessel from the second officer until absolutely sure the tanker's position was a safe one.

While in the chart room I noticed that my coffee was a milky white color, not its usual dark brown, and I began wondering what could be wrong with it. By this time my fellow watchstanders—unlicensed crew members—had relieved the off-going crew, so that our now terminated friends were below, probably curled up cozily in their bunks. I called the second officer into the chart room, asking him what was wrong with the pot of coffee.

"Why?" he asked.

I said, "Look at the coffee—there's something different about it."

To which he replied: "I don't know what the hell's wrong with it, but that certainly doesn't look like coffee." I told him to get the rest of the pot that was on the bridge and bring it back here, so that we could examine it in good light. In the meantime I carefully sniffed my cup, coming to the conclusion that it contained a poisonous, corrosive substance we used to strip rust off steel. It was called OSPHO, an acronym for some powerful chemical. Returning, the second officer and I discussed the matter at length, and he concurred that this wasn't pure coffee, but rather, a brew containing the stuff I had sniffed.

Under normal conditions I would now have called the ship's captain, for it was obvious somebody had it in for me. However Captain Bob was on one of his trips to the land of inebriation, so it would be impossible to deal with this situation via normal legal channels. I told the second officer I would take the count of the vessel, my customary duty, but that before he retired, I wanted him to go below and rouse those two deckhands, who I was sure were responsible for this attempted poisoning.

Within fifteen minutes the second officer arrived back on the bridge with the two co-conspirators in tow. I now planned to engage them in a war of mental torment, so I began by telling them how sorry I was to have fired them, for really, I *did* appreciate all their hard work. In fact I had wondered about this the previous night, and felt I had perhaps been premature in my decision. I said I suspected they came from some kind of dysfunctional backgrounds, so they probably had good cause to be heavy drinkers from time to time. I allowed that I could perhaps accommodate such behavior in the future; but I really wanted to have a heart-to-heart talk with them about the whole situation. I then explained that my background had been a relatively stable one, and that when family problems surfaced—I felt we were all family on this ship—why we would generally sit down over a cup of coffee and hash things out in a friendly way.

With that preamble completed, I suggested that they come onto the bridge so we could all grab a cup of java and chat a bit, seeing whether we could arrive at some agreement, by which they might be permitted to stay on board. I then picked up the coffee pot, pouring them two cups of the corrosive hot brew, while I carefully held mine in front of me, most already discarded. I now continued my discussion about life's little discrepancies; and after two or three minutes, casually asked why they didn't like the coffee, since they hadn't yet taken it to their lips. In a vain search for excuses both tripped over their words, one saying he didn't drink coffee, the other mumbling some other stupidity. In a less jovial manner I began to hone in on the mark, reminding them more firmly of how my family had dealt with problems—how our peacemaking process *always* concluded with a cup of coffee consumed by all. And that if they couldn't agree to have a coffee with me today, why *I* couldn't see my way to keeping them on board! I reminded them of their fondness for beverages, and how coffee was less harmful than alcohol. Raising my cup, as though in a toast, I said, "Let's make peace." The second officer was standing off in the dark—I could see only his silhouette—but I was sure he was appreciating the drama here!

My toast of course went unanswered, so I abruptly fired the scoundrels again, sending both down to their bunks below. Of course I did not tell them I was aware of their plot, wishing to leave the door open for more possible torment. If they felt I was 100% sure, they would remain vigilant for the rest of the voyage. I felt inside that I wasn't quite done with them yet. I was a cat with a couple of mice, and still thoroughly miffed, because these mice could easily have killed me. It took great restraint on my part not to be physical, which would have resulted in the loss of my license and livelihood, for which I'd worked so hard from a young age.

So I simply left the door ajar for more revenge, which I was happily able to obtain in rather short order. For word drifted up almost like a vapor from crew's quarters, teaching me some interesting things about these two poisoners manqués. It was particularly useful to learn that they had a rather large cache of alcohol secretly stowed on board.

Typically on a return voyage to the U.S., the ship's skipper handed out individual customs declaration forms to all on board, where crew members could list any items or products purchased abroad. These forms were filled out and signed by each crew member, then handed to the captain before we returned to the States. Once the customs agents boarded the vessel, the skipper would hand over these declarations for their perusal and for the payment of duties, if any were required. Agents occasionally spot-checked a crew member departing the vessel to see if he was carrying any foreign, undeclared goods. The main goal was to deter smuggling, especially of drugs and alcohol.

Inasmuch as our captain was out of commission most of the voyage, this duty now fell to me, and having heard about the cases of alcohol, I strongly suspected our scalawags would try smuggling them ashore. So acting on behalf of the captain, I had all customs forms filled out and returned to me ASAP. My two tormentors returned theirs promptly, with the statement "nothing to declare" written across the face of the documents. We were still several days from port, but I now knew I possessed something I could use to have them convicted of a crime. Smuggling is not regarded favorably by the U.S. government, and I realized it would seriously compromise these guys' future in the Merchant Marine. Getting caught would likely bring heavy fines and possible imprisonment, which suited me just fine.

About two days before reaching American waters, I managed to kickstart the captain's sobering process, so that on arrival he might be visible to port officials as a somewhat viable component of the vessel. After he was sober, I handed him all the customs declarations for the entire ship, which he would then give the agents when they boarded in Jacksonville. At about the same time, the two party animals came to me privately, asking if they might change their declarations. Apparently they were now getting a little nervous, learning that at least a few crew members on board thought highly enough of me that they might betray them, passing on their intended smuggling plan to the authorities. So here they were, asking for new declaration forms, which I duly gave them and which they filled out and returned to me. On these declarations they listed numerous cases of alcohol, obviously deciding to pay duties.

After they left my office, I took these second declaration forms and carefully shredding them in my hands, flung them out my porthole and upon the waters, watching the little white flakes loll placidly on the ocean's surface, before disappearing. A broad smile strode across my face. So far as I was concerned, they had made their true declaration, and they were going have to live and die with it. I wasn't about to start having every crew member change declarations at a whim.

Upon arrival in Jacksonville the customs agents performed their usual clearance procedures and things went smoothly, i.e., without any discussions. The agents left the ship, satisfied that all duties had been handed over by any individuals making declarations. Having notified the captain to hire two additional deckhands in replacement of the two I'd fired, I had also asked him to delay paying the two offgoing degenerates until the day after our arrival in port. Our intended stay was to be three days, which I knew would create some frustration in them. I told the skipper to tell them that he was waiting on money from the steamship agent.

As soon as our ship was cleared by Customs and Immigration, my two friends went ashore, presumably staying in a nearby hotel. They knew their replacements were already on board and that they wouldn't be paid till the next day. On the morning of the second day I informed the second officer to keep his eyes peeled, watching for the return of the two fired deckhands. The dock at the Hess Oil Terminal near Drummond Point was a lengthy one, extending about a mile into the St. John's River—one of the longest I'd seen. With the dock being that long, I would have plenty of time to make sure I was on deck and visible to the two returning comrades.

As they came on board, they sneered and laughed in my direction, skipping along like schoolboys to go and get paid by the captain. Without witnesses in the vicinity, I walked over, casually mentioning to them that they were sure lucky the Customs guys had decided not to charge them duty on their alcohol! I made sure that no one else heard me say this. At that point the liquor was still in the ship's forward section, and these guys were on their way to the aftersection. They obviously figured—for it wasn't unusual—that the Customs officials had simply decided, "Forget it—you don't have to pay duties." Which in at least 50% of cases did happen, for agents sometimes didn't care. This was known to all crew members. In my private conversation, while we were walking aft, I also told the pair that a Customs agent who had boarded the ship was a good friend of mine and that I'd asked if he could overlook any specific duty charges, "particularly with you guys." I said, "I knew you'd be on the beach for a while, and low on cash, and that this would be helpful to you." I tried to convey that I wasn't the hard-hearted Captain Bly they had thought I was. In actuality I was setting them up for the kill, aware that after getting paid off, they would have to walk the length of the ship right past the gangway, where myself, the second officer, and the ship's bosun would be working. They would have to walk the length of the ship because they had unfortunately stored their cases of booze in the *forward* end of the vessel. Why hadn't they simply taken them off earlier? Probably it was inconvenient—for one thing they didn't have a car. And usually you don't remove that stuff till your personal luggage is unloaded, and since we had arrived so late at night, they had also been tired, putting it off until they were rested.

After going forward and collecting all their cases of alcohol, which they had painted red for camouflage to avoid paying duties, they stacked them up by the gangway—about ten cases in all. They were just about to proceed down that gangway carrying the first case or two, when I hollered: "Stop! I want to see what those are!" Having been paid, they were no longer members of the ship's crew, so they decided to be as truculent as they wanted to be, looking at me as if to say, "Who the hell are you?" But I stepped between them and the cases of booze, and nose to nose, I said: "I hope this isn't what I think it is." The ship's bosun and second officer were close at hand, listening intently. "After all the trouble we had, you guys wouldn't have the audacity.... This couldn't be alcohol, could it?" They were speechless, their jaws dropped, their faces turned white, and they didn't know what to say, because they felt these cases had been declared and cleared. They stammered for an answer, but before they could speak, I instructed the bosun to cut the lashings off one of the cases and cut it open, because I wanted to check its contents. The two party animals vehemently objected, hollering "Don't cut the case!"; for it would be much harder to carry once the cardboard was breached.

So I asked again what was in the case. They said: "Alcohol. You *know* that. We declared it." Looking up from the case, I said: "Oh, did you? When did you do that?" They said: "We filled out the declarations and we gave them to you." And I said: "Yes, in fact, the bosun collected them from you and gave them to me." Then I asked: "Bosun, do you or the second officer recall seeing anything declared on these mens' customs forms?"

Naturally they responded in the negative, leaving the two fellows crying like wounded jackals, screaming that they had filled out subsequent, revised declarations. With palms open and extended slightly away from my body, I said, "I don't recall you ever handing in another set of declarations." They now got red in the face, steaming hot, doing exactly what I'd hoped they would do. They shouted at me and the second officer, and said something like: "We don't care. This is our booze and we're takin' it!"

So I ordered the second mate and the bosun to stand off and let them carry their alcohol onto the dock. Now they had become smugglers, and I was ready to spring the trap. At the bottom of the gangway there was a four-wheel luggage cart onto which they quickly loaded their booze and suitcases. There was also a bicycle there which the dockman used for transportation up and down the dock. This bike was the sole property of the refinery and the dockman, and as a courtesy could be used by a ship's chief officer or captain. I watched the two smugglers carefully stack their things on the four-wheel cart and start on a one-mile trek toward shore. Within a minute or two—I thought I'd give them a fair head start—I went to the bottom of the gangway, hopped on the bike, and headed down the dock. As I passed them, toiling arduously across these heavy creosote planks, I indicated that they'd better hurry if they were going to beat the Customs agents who were on their way. Of course I was about to make a phone call at the end of the dock, letting U.S. Customs know that I had two hot leads for them. Reaching the end of the dock, I was amused to see that the pair not only had a car, but also a couple of women they had obviously begun entertaining the night before. You could see that they were planning to keep entertaining them for the next two to three weeks.

When the two men got to within a half mile of the car, they began shouting as loudly as they could, their voices shrill and panicky, demanding that the women open the trunk to effect a quicker departure. Of course I scribbled down the car's license number. These guys were stumbling and sweating profusely, pushing the loaded cart ever closer to their getaway vehicle. And meanwhile, I had gotten to within 100 feet of a phone booth, soon braking there and dialing up my friends at the Customs office. It was exhilarating to watch the crazed fellows throw case after case into the back of the car, screaming and shouting noisily to "hurry, hurry"—and at the same time, trying to explain to the ladies why they were in such a rush.

As if on the old "Beat the Clock" show, they jumped into the back seat with the women up front, then the car sped away, its trunk lid still popped open and one case falling into the road. Dirt and dust flew out in great volumes as they spun their wheels to get onto the pavement. With a loud screech the rubber zipped off the sand, and off they went.

About thirty seconds later the Customs people arrived, and I pointed to the cloud of dust still in the air, telling them that the birds had just flown the coop, and giving them their license number. I then sat down and waited. After composing myself somewhat, I called my family to check in and see how everybody was doing at home; and while still on the phone, I saw the Customs vehicle pull up with these four people crammed into the back. The two agents got out and asked me if I could identify these people. I walked over to the back window, looking up and down very carefully, drawing out the moment as long as I could. Then I told the Customs officer in the driver's seat: "These are my two ex-shipmates, terminated for dereliction of duty and being found drunk on board a number of times."

To which the officer replied: "We'll stop and see you before you sail, and fill you in on their punishment." I later learned that the co-conspirators had each been fined $5,000, along with the women. In addition the two ex-crew members lost their seamens' documents and were henceforth never allowed to sail again, which constituted a rather light sentence. (Smuggling could put you in jail for years.) But in my mind I felt that at that point that I'd finally pulled the box out from under the hangman's noose!

Chapter 9

Returning as Captain Orton to KGB Land

WORKING under incompetent or incapacitated captains, like Captain Bob, and sometimes acting as a surrogate captain myself, I naturally thought quite often of attaining the top spot myself. In order to qualify for such a promotion, especially when a company showed interest in you for this higher capacity, you first had to pass stringent exams given by the federal agency monitoring the Merchant Marine–i.e., the U.S. Coast Guard. But having the Coast Guard set standards for Merchant Marine officers was truly laughable—and it had not always been so. Prior to World War II all Merchant Marine officers and the Marine itself had been overseen by the Steamship Inspectors' Society, a quasi-governmental review board setting standards for vessel construction and for licensing of officers. When a fellow wished to position himself for upgrade, he not only took a written examination, but oral and on site exams as well.

During and just after World War II the Coast Guard initiated a political power grab, entrenching their viability in the eyes of the government. They would henceforth receive tax dollars, permitting them to become sole overseers of the Merchant Marine. The laughable part was that the Coast Guard then and now hasn't had vessels even approaching the size of Merchant ships they governed, nor the shipboard experience of the average Merchant officer. One should note that in the early part of World II the Merchant Marine was ultra-valuable to the American naval effort, and within weeks of the declaration of war, nearly every Merchant officer had gotten conscripted into the U.S. Navy, due to their working knowledge of navigation and seamanship. Meanwhile, hordes of farm boys and city slickers who had never seen a ship, much less salt water, joined the Navy. So officers were taken off Merchant ships and placed on combat ships, especially to navigate escort vessels. Due to the pressures of sudden expansion, they became a hot property.

The navy created during the war was thus composed of mainly inexperienced sailors, convoyed in large groups across the Atlantic and following ships ahead of them. The outside "picket ships" were manned by former Merchant officers, who did the navigating, shepherding these ninety-day wonders who had just climbed off farm tractors or vacated city offices across the ocean.

This wartime situation allowed the Coast Guard to make its bid for power. It could now argue that the Merchant Marine, shorn of experienced men, should be monitored and overseen by an authorized maritime authority, which they claimed themselves to be. So toward the end of the war Congress passed laws putting the Coast Guard over the Merchant Marine, and supplanting the old Steamship Society. The Coast Guard could henceforth make recommendations on ship construction, as well as supervise the licensing process for officers. Oddly, its inspectors were not required to possess the same credentials or experience themselves. So it would be common to have a Coast Guard inspector board a Merchant ship in almost total ignorance of its everyday workings, especially from an operational point of view. The largest Coast Guard vessels plying U.S. coastal waters ranged to maybe 180 feet tops; yet this agency was involved in accrediting officers who commanded or at least had heavy responsibilities on ships fifty times their size. That would be roughly akin to a neighborhood bicycle repairman evaluating a Boeing or NASA engineer.

Coast Guard examinations *were* extensive, but much of the questioning was plain irrelevant. To give an example, during my impending examination for master, one question in the written format would be: How do you determine whether horses you are carrying on board are thirsty? I am not kidding the reader! I couldn't understand the significance of such a question, when the only equine species we generally encountered on board were horses' posteriors who had gotten their positions by leverage with unions and with incompetent Coast Guard officials, or by kissing up to company staff, creating problems for the rest of us. By the way the answer to that bizarre exam question: if you put water in front of the horses and they drank it, then they were indeed thirsty! Not that I wish to underestimate qualifications and qualities it took to become a Merchant Marine captain; but such questions *did* make you laugh out loud while taking such a test.

The Coast Guard had abandoned the old Steamship-type verbal interrogations of a licensed applicant, for that procedure would be like speaking in two different languages. Due to the gulf in knowledge and nomenclature, the inspector simply wouldn't know whether an applicant was answering questions correctly or not.

All this notwithstanding, I decided at my wife's urging that as soon as my vacation began, I would sit for the master's or captain's examination, just as I had done for prior exams (second officer, chief officer, etc.). These tests generally lasted four days to a week, and eight hours a day, covering a gamut of topics—shipboard sanitation, celestial and terrestrial navigation, cargo-handling and operations, administrative or admiralty law questions (these sections on international law being particularly prominent on the master's examination), health and hygiene, first aid and medical treatment for the injured, weather conditions, and so on. But the whole experience was artificial and contrived. Sitting in a classroom, how could you put into written words the way you handled a lifeboat in heavy surf? How could you show your *actual* proficiency in a demanding environment? These were problems I wondered about at the time.

When I arrived home, I was unaware that the master's examination was scheduled for the following day—quite a jolt! The result was that I had little or no time for preparation. On my last voyage I'd been both chief officer and most of the time, de facto captain as well, and was therefore, exhausted. So I fully expected to fail this examination my first time around. But I felt it was worth a try because it would furnish insights on the types of questions I'd get on the next exam. Of course such tests routinely change, but at least I would know the general flavor. By the way, one could only take these examinations twice. If you failed to pass on a second attempt, you would find yourself stuck at your current rank.

So with my wife supporting me, I decided to give it a shot. Susie was truly an asset in encouraging me to move ahead expeditiously in rank. She had always been helpful on previous exams, keeping the kids away from me during study times, and generally providing a real psychological boost.

Still, I started this exam fully expecting not to pass. If you flunked any section, you were immediately ejected, and there were a couple of sections each day, graded immediately afterwards.   After   passing the fourth section, I began to see a slim possibility that I might actually make it through this ordeal, though five more sections, some very difficult (especially when you hadn't prepared enough) still awaited me. Every night that I came home as a viable candidate for the next day seemed exciting, and that excitement level rose as I got closer to the finish line. There were three other candidates sitting for the exam, but by the time I arrived at the last two sections, only one in his mid-fifties remained, the other two having been axed. During the initial part of the examination the inspector had seemed cool and distant with me, but now he warmed up a bit, beginning to call us by our first names.

This helped psychologically, for he seemed to have a newly-vested interest in seeing us pass. Not that he graded more leniently, but in a subtle way, he became a kind of cheerleader. When I left the classroom the evening before the last day, he called me aside, exhorting me to stay focused and declaring that the next day's section would be very difficult. In other words he wanted me to keep a steady hand on the mental tiller.

Returning home to review the following day's material, I worked well into the wee hours, trying to control myself and concentrate on the task at hand. I admit that my anxiety level was accentuated when Apex Marine called in the morning before I left to complete my examination, asking whether I had passed and received my master's license. When and if that occurred, they said, they wanted to promote me to captain within their company.

Arriving at the exam room, I somehow maintained composure, and when the paper was dropped on my desk, I attacked it like a ravenous lion, finishing well ahead of the other candidate. I went forward to hand in the paper and the instructor asked if I perhaps needed to review it, obviously concerned at the speed with which I'd finished. He asked me a second time whether I was ready to hand it in now. I answered that I was. He then instructed me to leave the room and remain in an adjoining waiting area. So I sat there for what felt like days (maybe only fifteen minutes in actual time); and finally from another doorway leading out into the corridor a young woman came in and said: "Congratulations, Captain Orton," adding: "The inspector wanted me to make sure we spelled your name properly on your unlimited tonnage, ocean master's license." (Good for any ship of any size in the world.)

Letting all my pent-up tension release, I leapt up and ran excitedly to the phone to call my wife, telling her the good news. Then I rang up the company, informing them that I had just received my captain's license. And I couldn't wait to get home to hug Susie, whose encouragement had been so crucial to my success.

I never found out what happened to the other candidate, but my guess is that he made out fine, too. In our conversations during breaks he seemed pretty astute.

About a month later, in late March 1979, the company called, with news that they were assigning me as permanent captain on *The Golden Endeavor*, one of seven ships built in San Diego as "San Clemente-class supertankers." I was to join the vessel in Port Arthur, Texas. We would then take it out to sea, flushing the tanks of heavy accumulations of crude oil, wax, sediment, and asphalt-type hydrocarbons. We had to clean the tanker thoroughly before making another grain-laden voyage to the U.S.S.R. of the late Brezhnev era. This assignment was right up my alley, as I had done the same thing three years before, but on a ship about one-fifth the size of this monster.

We had hard work in store—a good three weeks worth. I wheeled the ship to an offshore reef, anchoring her in international waters off the Texas coast. This was the "Flower Garden Reef," a protrusion coming off the Gulf of Mexico's ocean floor. Here we could lay an anchor, holding the ship in place while we finished cleaning out our cargo tanks.

Once we had completed that job, we were given instructions to proceed to the mouth of the Mississippi, whereupon we went up river to load our ship at grain elevators just north of New Orleans. After about seven to ten days we finished loading, though because of the ship's size we couldn't fill it completely with our cargo of grain. The river's depth wouldn't have permitted us to negotiate it with such a heavy load on board.

Instead, we stuffed it about three-quarters full, then headed out toward an area familiar to me—the Mediterranean Sea and thence through the Dardanelles, passing the heart of Constantinople and into the treacherous Bosporus Straits, particularly difficult to navigate because of heavy currents. For a huge ship so deeply loaded down, extreme caution was a necessity here, for we were vulnerable to these underwater currents. During this transit through the Bosporus I remained super-vigilant.

But after entering the Black Sea, a sinking feeling invaded me—for my communications to the West were now cut off. Communist authorities required all shipboard radio transmissions to be made only on their approval, something we had agreed on before this voyage.

Speaking of Communism and of the Cold War era still in high gear, I must explain that while in New Orleans I had had a couple of visitors join me on the ship late one afternoon, identifying themselves as working for the Federal government. At first I surmised that they were health inspectors, OSHA inspectors, customs, or immigration officials—something of that nature. I greeted them, pouring out cups of coffee, and initially their conversation was rather anodyne, mainly questions about our loading process. Eventually, however, they opened up, indicating that they worked with the CIA. They then asked whether I was interested in helping them in one of many different possible capacities while over in Russia. I asked them point-blank what they were looking for, and they said they needed to collect some information to update their files on Soviet personnel in the port of Odessa. I asked for more specifics, and they took out a book, a kind of lunch menu thing, telling me that whatever I selected would bring some sort of compensation. They were looking for material in several areas, and each tidbit garnered would be rewarded accordingly, as indicated on this menu list. There were different jobs they wanted undertaken, some of which seemed too risky for a married man and father; others, however, appeared more reasonable and easier to negotiate successfully. So I indicated to them a couple of different subjects or areas I'd try to take care of for them. They made it clear that I was under no compunction to aid them and that my choices were purely voluntary.

Then they opened another briefcase, showing me a photo album of known Russian or Ukrainian KGB agents. They said I could keep the album for review, because it might come in handy before my arrival. When not in my hands, they asked that it be kept in the ship's safe at all times, and I had no problem with that. To destroy the album I must burn it, then place its ashes in a weighted bag, dropping it into deep waters. This type of spying might sound like a serious thing to undertake, but at least I knew I would have diplomatic immunity over there and therefore, couldn't be arrested, given that I would be the highest-ranking American official in Odessa (there was no American attaché or consul in that city).

So I had my duties set forth, and was then provided with a couple of unusual coffee cups equipped with little cameras in the bottoms. Any time you lifted up the cup horizontally, it clicked a noiseless picture. In the bottom of the cup all you saw was what looked like nothing more than a dark dimple. Part of my assignment was to photograph certain individuals, as well as harbor locations or installations. After the CIA men completed their spiel, giving me the hardware I needed, they left, and I never saw them again before my trip to the U.S.S.R. They had provided instructions as to where to mail the coffee cups on my return, which again I had to keep in the ship's safe. And that was that...

We had now entered the Black Sea and as noted, I felt something of a cold curtain descend over the whole ship. I felt very distanced from the rest of the world, and was particularly concerned about my family. I knew the company had exercised great confidence in me by assigning me to a ship of this magnitude and for a trip into Communist territory, where all decisions would be made without assistance from the home staff. This was one of the first times that I really felt the weight of my duties as captain, and also experienced some doubts. Previously, I had never been cocky, but generally confident. All the cockiness in me had been sapped out by prior experiences I've described here. There was a certain cold reality to this job that took focus and concentration, and little time or space was left over for self-adulation.

I remember when I originally joined the ship as captain, and we had left Port Arthur, Texas for the open sea and our upcoming tank cleaning session, how the helmsman, a guy in his early fifties named Willis, asked if he could speak to me on the bridge. Normally ship's crew don't get in a conversation with a captain unless the latter initiates it. They usually keep a distance. We had our talk, and Willis stated that he was surprised I looked so youthful. He asked my age, and when I answered that I was in my early thirties, he said: "That's quite an awesome responsibility you have!" He was perhaps concerned for his own welfare, wondering whether my background and experience sufficed for such an important first voyage. But I also wondered whether he might be trying to patronize me, in order to procure special treatment later on.

After he mentioned my huge responsibility, I spoke to this Willis, with three other officers standing nearby, saying something like the following to him: "Willis, what you and I do here today—as awesome as it may seem to those on a ship of this size and a voyage of this intent—carries no future impact beyond the fact that in fifty years this tanker will either be cut up into razor blades (*many* razor blades), or lie at the bottom of the ocean! What transpires on this ship over the next three months will have little influence on the world's future. But I know somebody even younger than myself, my wife, who in the next three months will have an enormous impact on our future. She isn't in charge of a supertanker and thirty-five mens' lives, plus millions of dollars worth of cargo; but she does bear responsibility for the lives of two growing children, whom she will help mold and then launch into a future generation. Their lives and their childrens' lives will touch thousands of people. How does that responsibility compare with what we have to do today?" I think this labored answer fell rather unexpectedly on his ears and took him aback. He had probably expected something like, "Yeah, I'm an important guy, all right, and the boss, and everyone here will follow my orders, and we have great things to do...." From then on it was apparent to officers and unlicensed men on board that my focus was on doing the job, not making it larger than life.

By the time we'd entered the Black Sea, I had a pretty clear idea of who we had on board—who could be relied on and who could not; who were the comparative and not so comparative kooks. Several unlicensed crewmen, some in their late twenties or early thirties, were obviously headed for trouble—they had already had brushes with me—and they remained in my mind as potential problems once we got ashore in Russia.

Approaching the port of Odessa by night, I found its designated anchorage area filled with ships, and due to the size of our vessel, felt it imprudent to anchor too close to the other, smaller vessels there. After repeatedly calling port control on the designated frequency, requesting their insights as to where we ought to anchor, and getting no answer, I simply picked a spot on the chart that looked like good holding ground, about a mile further out, yet near enough to the port.

On our previous voyage to Russia, when I was with Gulf, we had never anchored offshore. We simply arrived and went straight into the dock. So this part of the Soviet adventure was new to me. As soon as we dropped anchor, I noted on our radar the approach of two vessels from two different directions, both lacking lights. This made me worry immediately about pirates, so I prepared the crew for a potential boarding situation. However, I should have realized that piracy probably didn't flourish in Communist Russia!

As the craft came closer, we noticed that these were Soviet military gunboats. Slowly circling our ship from about seventy-five feet away, they shone a small searchlight on our ship's nameplate and on the gangway we'd rigged over the side. Using a megaphone and in broken English, they then shouted several times: "Gangway up, gangway up!" I duly instructed the chief officer to raise the gangway and later learned the reason for this order. Soviet gunboats patrolled these anchorage areas in order to arrest any swimmers attempting to reach a ship and defect to the West. Once on board they became part of that ship's sovereignty. Our vessel was indeed an extension of American soil, and those who might try for asylum could be a problem for me, too.

These Soviet gunboats had excessively loud diesel engines, aggravating enough to us; but they also shone their search lights into the ship's bridge, getting on the microphone and harassing us day and night with Communist propaganda, to the point where we were quite frazzled after being anchored for four days. I now decided to hatch a plan which would hopefully keep those gunboats at a greater distance from our tanker. Very carefully I constructed a device I felt would do the trick, taking two four-by-four wooden posts, cutting them down to about a foot long each, and connecting these two modified posts with a heavy piece of baling wire fifty to sixty feet long. Then I lowered one end of the contraption into the water and as a gunboat came by us that night, I threw the other end out as far as I could. The wire was suspended at a very shallow depth under the water's surface.

As the Soviet boat passed between the two floating pieces of wood, the suspended wire underneath was dragged into its propellers, causing them to be caught up in the wire, until the propeller shaft simply sheared off and the boat drifted away, its skipper crying loudly for help from one of the Russian tugboats. They now needed a tow to shore. From then on these gunboats never approached our ship so closely again, keeping at least a quarter of a mile distant. And they never accused me of anything either.

After about a week a small pilot boat arrived in daytime, and with no prior warning, announced that port authorities wanted a Russian pilot to board our ship. As we have seen earlier, these pilots were maritime experts able to handle tides, currents, and other local knowledge in order to help dock a ship. Use of such caddies of the sea was common practice. So once the pilot was aboard, I asked if we were going to dock, figuring there should now be space for it. He replied that we weren't going to do that yet. Despite his limited English vocabulary we conversed about what the Russians *were* trying to do. Apparently they simply wanted to move our ship a short distance, then re-anchor it, and I asked why. The Russian pilot could give no logical answer. For a whole week we'd been waiting for the one berth available to take a ship of this size. Never had such a large tanker been seen in Odessa, and even that one potential berth would make a tight squeeze. But concerning the pilot's request, I told him in good Cold War style that he could "go to hell" and that he should get off my ship immediately. He was simply not going to budge us a quarter of a mile for no good reason, charging our company for a needless move that would cost many thousands of dollars.

Ignoring me, the pilot gave an order to our helmsman, which I immediately countermanded, telling Willis simply to disregard this guy. The helmsman followed my order. Plainly infuriated, and in a voice that was many decibels above loud, the Russian pilot screamed something on our ship radio to a port commissioner or other official. A minute later he shoved the microphone over to me, saying: "You talk." I got on the radio, identifying the tanker and myself, and asked with whom I was speaking. The answer? Dimitri L. Bazarov[10], captain of the port of Odessa, and head man in charge of all maritime operations here. Bazarov said he wanted our ship moved. His English was very good, and again I asked why he wanted the move. He gave me some fuzzy answer, which I told him I could see through; and I think we both decided at that moment that we wouldn't be friends for the next three months. I asked Bazarov when our berth would be available and he said: "Within the next three or four days." I handed the microphone back to the pilot, there was some conversation in Russian, and then he re-boarded his boat and left.

Three or four days later he was back, guiding us into the dock site; but unfortunately, the tanker didn't fit. It was my responsibility to see that our ship was safely in port, so I issued a vehement protest to Soviet port authorities, to the effect that I wouldn't permit us to remain in such a precarious position, unless they provided at *their* expense two tugboats to hold us here. After a lengthy argument I hauled out the charter party—the maritime term for the contract between cargo consignees (the Russians) and the shipper. I also filed a formal written protest. I think they were learning not to underestimate me because of my youth. Anyway, they reluctantly agreed, and for the rest of our stay these two tug boats stood by our tanker, keeping it from falling away from the dock, and preventing damage to either the ship or port facility.

As soon as we got the gangway down, the first person to greet me was Captain Bazarov himself. Bazarov entered my office and stateroom with a broad smile and a handshake, openly insincere to me after our previous conversation. The Communist dignitary acted as though we'd been friends for years, but the hand he offered me seemed to be one he wanted filled with cigarettes and other black market goodies. I knew that for the next three months and at every opportunity, Soviet officials of whatever capacity who boarded our ship would try to intimidate me. For these high officials—the only people who could get by armed guards protecting our ship from asylum-seekers—blackmail would be a routine procedure, in order to obtain western products of choice. In fact it became a daily joke that there was always someone to see me from some damned Russian department or other.

I remember, for instance, Soviet Agriculture Department personnel coming on board, telling me we couldn't eat American meat while in Russia and that if I needed meat, I should simply order it through

---

[10]   This is a pseudonym.

the Russian ship chandler or purveyor. One agricultural bigwig emphasized that if we failed to comply, he would place a seal on our frozen meat locker in the galley area, rather like the wire gizmo you see on water meters. I simply laughed at the threat, which angered him greatly. I said that they could put on any seal they wanted, that they could weld the locker shut, but that we would simply cut off whatever device they used. I emphasized that I and my crew were *not* going to be subjected to eating Russian meat. Ironic, I added more or less, "that every day when you come here, you seem to have no problem at all scarfing down lunch, enjoying the nice prime rib and turkey you get, and now you want us to eat Russian food? There's no meat in the city of Odessa fit to be consumed by me and my crew! And let me remind you," I continued, "I've been here before, and I've seen your fine Krasny hotel, and I have sampled from that scrumptious, mouthwatering menu; and if you're looking for a handout or an opportunity to put something over on me, so that you can walk away with some cigarettes, you'd better look again, because you've come to the wrong ship! You need to take your carcass back to Bazarov and tell him that we won't put up with this stuff. If your officials expect to have an open door to enjoy meals fit for a king, then they'd better get their act together."

Of course I knew that everything in the Soviet Union was government-operated and run. The steamship agents, interpreters, and other officials who came on board were all under Dimitri Bazarov in the hierarchy here. I also happened to know that Bazarov was eminent KGB and something akin to the centerfold of the photo album I'd destroyed on my way over here. I knew that he was the boss in charge of the entire KGB operation in Odessa, and that one shouldn't underestimate his extensive power base.

Bazarov was henceforth more careful in how he dealt with me. He made sure at every opportunity to proffer gifts and perks, trying to make my stay in Russia as comfortable as possible. These perks included keeping a car and chauffeur at my beck and call at all times. The car would literally stay parked with its driver on the dock near the bow of our ship. The chauffeur himself was another recognizable face in the KGB cast of characters that I had studied on the way here. The really fun part was the first time Bazarov took me down to see the big black sedan, standard issue for top Soviet officials. Just like an American used car salesman, he thumped the tires, and showed me how nice and comfortable it was. He then told me in front of Boris, the chauffeur, that unfortunately as nice as the car was, and as effective as Boris was as a driver, that he could not understand English. If I wanted to go anywhere, it would be best for me simply to point on the map of Odessa, and Boris would make sure I got there safe and sound. Bazarov also made available a private hotel suite, in case I had to conduct shore-side business with locals in the privacy of a conference room. And indeed, my first trip by car was to this Marisk Hotel. Boris was unctu-ously cordial, opening and closing all doors for me. On arrival he even offered to carry my attaché case, but I declined, not wanting him to touch anything I had on me. The hotel was not much to look at—three stories high and rather drab from the outside, reminding me of a hospi-tal one arrived at from the center entrance, with wings to the right and left. From the air it would form a capital I. In the center was a registra-tion desk where I was greeted by several flunkies. Boris had a brief dis-cussion with them in Russian, whereupon I was escorted to my new shoreside office/stateroom facility. The hotel manager spoke a little English and made a great effort to convey all of the room's amenities. This was of course a certified Intourist hotel, although I would find it split left and right—the one side a residence for Russian merchant mariners, put up here during vacation periods, as a home away from home; the other for westerners on official business in Russia, either businessmen or visiting dignitaries. This arrangement made it conven-ient for the KGB to monitor activities of anyone traveling in and out of Russia.

Being a member of the Soviet Merchant Marine meant you were part of the elite, but it also carried definite price tags. Every Russian ship that plied the oceans in this era had the typical staffing operations of all merchant ships, *plus* a political officer on board, whose title was "commissar." The commissar's duty was to protect the political integ-rity and interests of the Soviet Union, especially by keeping a ship's operations free from the menace of desertion. In almost every case the vessel's captain was not the commissar, but rather, subject to his or-ders. A commissar could literally pull a gun to stop defectors—he was fully authorized to use every method up to and including murder in order to prevent them from succeeding. When Russian seamen went ashore in prosperous western countries, especially the U.S., they were allowed to do so only in parties of one or two, and escorted by the commissar. These Soviet seamen knew that if they made any attempt to defect, there would be serious repercussions for their families at home—with long prison sentences a safe bet. It was not uncommon for both a husband and wife to be in the Merchant Marine, but under no circumstances could they sail together. Soviet authorities obviously believed the couple that sailed together could defect together.

The government would conduct frequent background checks on merchant mariners to determine whether they were politically qualified, i.e., loyal to the precepts of Communism. They also checked family backgrounds to make sure that any seamen considering asylum would leave possible hostages for authorities to put in prison. For example, the Party would know if a mother and father were still alive, and they would also know about siblings, children, and so on. They would check as well to see whether applicants were Communist Party members, and whether their family had any history of dissidence. In brief, it behooved Russian seamen traveling the world to ignore the bright lights of freedom and prosperity, and to toe the Party line.

That Soviet Merchant Marine was obviously habituated to spying, and Bazarov himself had come up via this career route. His English wasn't only excellent because he had studied it from youth. He had also been captain of a Russian merchant ship traveling regularly to the States from the 1960s, in order to pick up grain and other foodstuff cargoes. Bazarov's ship had appeared at some of the same grain elevators and ports where I had loaded cargoes. So he had definitely improved his English while on duty in these American port cities.

As one might expect, the hotel he located for me was bugged from top to bottom, and even an idiot would have realized that immediately. When you picked up the phone, those who monitored conversations were so amateurish that you heard their coughing or their recording machines being clicked on, as well as static in the background. There were occasions when just picking up the phone sent me into gales of laughter. Frequently I'd cue listeners into the number I was dialing; in case they misread it, I thought I'd just give it to them orally, so they wouldn't make a mistake and end up in Siberia for it. Of course I often dialed numbers selected at random. There were even times when I'd pick up the phone and play music from my tape recorder, so they could enjoy recent material by the Bee Gees or Fleetwood Mac. (The Russians had a voracious appetite for western music, matching songs to artists better than I could.)

My room in the hotel was two floors up from the lobby and close to the main staircase. In each central part of an upper floor, there was an open sitting area, again, rather like in an American hospital. There you could sit on two or three stuffed couches. But a floor monitor always lurked nearby, generally a woman, whose job was to make sure that people staying in opposite wings never crossed that neutral no-man's land. In other words Russian merchant mariners couldn't traipse into the sector occupied by western dignitaries, and likewise, westerners could not enter the area inhabited by Russian seamen, unless escorted by a commissar.

The chief hall commissar I knew—separating western from Russian components of the hotel—was a woman who, it turned out, had a fascinating story inside. She was elderly, probably in her early seventies, and seemed like a typical Russian grandmother. This made her account all the more surprising. One day I was leaving my suite, where I liked to relax a while during days when I was away from the ship. I used the phone here to call the ship's officers. This was also my jumping-off base, from which I could make visits or examine Russian society both for the CIA and my own edification. I guess the hotel became a kind of excuse I handed Bazarov's boys, so that I could travel around and absorb Odessan ways.

Anyway, on this particular occasion, as I was leaving my suite, this older woman anxiously called me over. I noticed that she had first looked carefully up and down the hallway, as if crossing a busy thoroughfare; and I noticed, too, that she called me in English, which though heavily accented, turned out to be easy to understand. She started by asking if I could bring some Chiclets for her grandchildren. I thought she was a kind lady, and decided to sit down with her for a while at the table where she spent her days on the government's payroll. We talked briefly about her grandkids, then she heaved a big sigh, and I wondered whether she was feeling ill. That sigh was the prelude to a story she was obviously aching to unburden from herself.

Long ago, she said, she had fallen in love with an American—before I was born. This American man had come to Odessa in her wartime youth as part of the U.S. Army. As she started telling the story, a tear rolled down her cheek, obviously catching her off guard. She nonetheless smiled and said, "I thought I wouldn't cry again." I guess I reminded her somewhat of this American army guy from her youth, for I was probably about the same age as he had been then, and as she soon told me, physically we also resembled each other. A Chicagoan, he had been part of a military attaché group in Russia during our Lend-Lease period. American military equipment was being shipped in to aid the Soviet war effort, and because the lady was a Red Army soldier and could speak English—I never found out where she had learned it—she was assigned as an interpreter for this young American lieutenant. In that high Stalinist era she naturally avoided any outward display of emotions for the visitor, but in fact, both secretly confessed to deep mutual feelings, and an intense relationship obviously developed.

One day, however, she arrived at the office where she worked with the Americans, and her beau was absent—he hadn't come in that day. One of the junior officers explained to her that the fellow had been called back to another post in the States—a sudden and abrupt departure. The poor lady was crushed, and she never saw or heard from him again. She presumed—and it sounded like the right explanation—that the Russian secret police, having nosed out the affair, ordered an immediate recall of her lieutenant. All Communist authorities had to do was demand that the American consul eject one of their countrymen as a spy, and he was gone.

The emotional hall commissar finished her story by giving me the man's name, hoping I would look him up on my return to the U.S. A couple days later I returned to the hotel with my briefcase full of chewing gum, and she was visibly moved. Her first problem was where to hide these "Chiclets"—her clothes being the first resort. I remembered that ironically Mr. Wrigley's city was Chicago.

When I got back to the U.S., I went to the downtown Buffalo library and taking out a Chicago area phonebook, found nothing under the man's name. I'd had every intention of following up on her wishes to locate him and convey her loving thoughts; but I came up with absolutely nothing.

Speaking of wartime, later during my stay in Odessa, a friend I made provided me an English translation of a Russian history text on "the Great War," which for them was World War II. Used in the teaching of university English, as well as for history classes, the book gave an interesting perspective of how Russia perceived its wartime allies. The parts of the book that made sense were those showing utter hatred for the Germans, due to their war crimes. In places like Odessa the Nazi occupation had been truly horrific. Of course the book said nothing about Stalin's own extensive purges, making Ukrainians hate him to this day. But it really became skewed when the authors called Churchill a double-dealing traitor. They figured that Churchill along with FDR had promised Stalin they would invade Western Europe via France in the spring of 1943. We know of course that they decided instead to come up the Italian boot from Sicily, but that wasn't what the Russians desired. The book basically declared that the huge number of Russian deaths in that war would have been greatly diminished had their allies not colluded with the Germans, allowing them to devastate the Soviet Union. (Nothing here on Stalin's poor preparations, his purges of top army personnel during the '30s, his Nazi-Soviet non-aggression pact of 1939, etc.) They argued that only when it looked like Russia would survive did the Allies decide on the D-Day operation—jackals tardily snatching up some of the victory laurels. I laughed at this stuff, but even well-informed Russians bought into it.

The term "Russian" that I use here is of course a convenient short-hand, as the Soviet Union was obviously composed of many different races, ethnicities, or nationalities. In Odessa you quickly learned to ascertain which nationality you were talking to, since mistaking a Ukrainian for a Russian was a great insult. A westerner like myself could to some degree exploit these ethnic rifts in a seemingly mono-lithic land, for Ukrainians still considered the Russians almost an oc-cupying force.

Moving back to the hotel I used, along with Soviet seamen in that one part were the Intourist guides, young men and women from all parts of the country. Their job was to herd westerners around Odessa, meeting their groups at the airport, supervising boarding of buses, and then watching over them as though they were paroled murderers. All Intourist guides were Communist Party members, having passed strin-gent review procedures to ensure that they could spout the Party line to perfection. They were trained to answer in a politically correct manner any question westerners might pose. They were also allowed to accept gratuities, but in a discreet way, and in fact, were already well paid, relative to other Russian incomes. In this supposedly egalitarian country a Russian doctor would earn maybe a hundred rubles a week, where Intourist guides just out of college and still in their early twen-ties typically pulled down three or four times that much.

Such inequities abounded in the Soviet Union, which never ceased to amaze me. For openers one could mention stores in Odessa that were off limits to virtually all locals. These places conducted their business solely in hard currency, and the only people allowed in were the highest Soviet government officials, or western tourists and digni-taries. Inside, one found common luxuries from the West, and the few employees who worked there were themselves a privileged caste, sons and daughters of eminent government officials, etc. Russians wishing to enter had to show special identification, and even westerners needed to obtain a pass from their hotel or Intourist guide in order to shop in stores that would be very average in the U.S. In Russia they were such a big thing that they were heavily guarded; you always saw at least one Red Army soldier outside, and two more as you walked through the doors.

Weapons on the hip were common pretty well everywhere in Russia. Our ship always had Soviet soldiers stationed about fifty feet away, and then at strategic intervals, in order to prevent prospective defectors from reaching us. The whole port area had a further security perimeter around it, keeping the public away. Naturally longshoremen permitted on the tanker had had *their* backgrounds carefully checked, exactly like the merchant seamen. If a Russian stevedore decided to defect, there was always at least one person in his family whom authorities could jail, or in some manner torment.

But as much as some longshoremen might have considered asylum, one should also remember that in their country they already lived like comparative kings, with easy access to black market items, due to their jobs. They were forever trying to negotiate for anything you had. Your teeshirt might say: "I'M A PIG'S SNOUT!, " and they would think that was marvelous. They also prized any kind of running shoes we had. I also knew a Soviet fellow who did everything he could to buy an American flag of ours. The flag meant nothing emotionally to him, but everything monetarily. Each day he would up the ante as to how much he would pay, and he never stopped pestering me about that flag.

Returning to the Intourist guides who lived in the hotel, I remember a day when I left the tanker to wander about on my own, and came upon a guided group. That day I'd simply refused the driver at the dock, waving my hand to indicate I wouldn't need him, and walked into the city on my own. Of course Boris might have followed me at some points, but he was basically left out of my plans. Remember that virtually all westerners the Russians saw were herded into groups and transferred from one spot to another by bus. If they walked, it would be no more than 50 or 100 yards; otherwise they were put back on the bus. Intourist guides faithfully counted and recounted these people, exactly as a rancher does his cattle.

So here I am, walking alone through Odessa's streets one summer day of 1979, clad in blue jeans and a white, striped polo shirt, and with prized Nikes on my feet, identifying me to the average Russian as someone not to be fooled with. To them I could *only* be a high Soviet official, or a westerner. And as noted, Soviet citizens were forbidden to engage in any conversation with us—making you understand how truly courageous dissidents of the era were; that is, unless an escorting Russian guide allowed it to occur. The Soviets were well educated in the serious ramifications that came from accosting tourists. Except for working situations such as on our ship, the average Russian in the street avoided you like some bacillus, knowing how much their government sought to insulate Soviet society from capitalist influences. The problem was that the country was getting so capital-crunched and starved for western currency that it became forced to open its borders for trade purposes. The Russians' need for basic food staples such as grain was another motivator. Interestingly, Russian stevedores conveyed to us that the reason they were getting this grain from the U.S. was because during World War II the Soviets had fed the Americans! This was a typical lie they had obviously heard, then passed along. Due to the undying efforts of the U.N. and worldwide embarrassment, the Americans had reluctantly agreed to repay the grain in a quantity worthy of Russia's wartime generosity! Some of these stories just slayed me. Maybe in their hearts the Russians didn't really believe them, but who knew?

So this was a quiet day for me in Odessa, and I ambled near the opera house they had built here as a replica of the famous Viennese opera house. Bombed during the war, the present version was probably reconstructed with partially Jewish or maybe even Nazi labor. I should add that Russians by and large seemed very anti-Semitic, as well as anti-black, for whom they had special contempt. Anyway by the Opera House I noticed a bus pull up, and immediately the doors opened, and a bunch of westerners began filing out. I'd seen these tourist buses before, but it was unusual to hear flawless American English coming out of passengers' mouths. Other buses generally contained Europeans—maybe French, Italians, or Danes, though not many Germans; due to their awful war memories, the Russians didn't exactly welcome German tourists with open arms. But in the main, Americans didn't choose to visit Russia, in lieu of a Florida or Paris vacation. Who would want to eat at the Krasny Hotel? And if by chance westerners visited once, what would induce them to return?

As soon as this American group offloaded, they arranged themselves in a non-conformist line of sorts. The young Intourist guide in her mid-twenties then descended, a mother hen escorting her chicks across the street to the opera house. At the same time she noted my presence, taking a good long look, trying to figure out who I was. Figuring I'd have some fun, I casually joined up with stragglers in the rear, striking up a conversation with two tourist couples at the end of the line, startled to hear my English. In one couple the husband was a Ford dealer from Michigan. Having told me where they were from, they asked where I was from, and I answered mysteriously: "That remains to be seen." They asked why I was traveling on my own here, while they were being constantly observed, counted, and directed about like figures in a video game. So I thought I'd play a little game of my own, giving these Americans a story to take home to friends and relatives. I knew they had paid big bucks to use wax toilet paper at the hotel and to consume bad meat, and to be shepherded around by Intourist guides. Having ducked their question as to who I was and what I was doing in the Soviet Union, I knew they might take me for some type of operative, one who might even try to enrol them in the gathering of clandestine information!

While the Intourist guide described the architectural or aesthetic qualities of the building before us, she kept watching me. She went on for nearly a half hour about the structure's unique lines and setting, and how the social and ideological fabric of the country factored in as well. Staying within the parameters of the Party line, her English was very good. Most of these Intourist guides were taught and trained by a professor of English at the University of Odessa, with whom I would strike up a close friendship, and who I will later describe.

Anyway, I began to perceive that this young lady was growing fearful of me. She knew that superiors looked over *her* shoulder, for "Big Brother"-type surveillance was obviously routine here. These spies would periodically come around to see if guides were correctly parroting Party dogma and acting in an appropriate way. But to stay mysterious, I purposely kept my distance from the guide. On a few occasions she started walking through the crowd so she could overhear my conversation with the Americans I'd befriended. But when the crowd walked a short distance over to a war monument, she continued to lecture—on the quality of Russian soldiers who had beaten back the Nazis here; and I continued to intermingle with a few more Americans on the group's periphery.

By now many in the group were gawking at me, wondering why I could tour Russia without an escort, when *they* were so closely guarded that even if they got up to go to the bathroom in the middle of the night—hotels generally lacking private ones—there would be someone watching in the hallway. In any event I now decided I'd act boldly to provide myself an evening's entertainment; so as soon as the guide had finished talking and was boarding these sheep back onto their bus, bound for the Krasny with its fine food and its crystal, I walked up to her, last in line, and addressing her by her first name, which I'd learned from the Americans, I said: "Natasha, I'd like to continue to stay with your people. Have you any problems with me riding the bus back to the hotel and remaining with the group through the evening, since I know your itinerary calls for dinner and entertainment at the Krasny Hotel?" Taken aback, perhaps because I knew so much about these planned activities, Natasha closed the bus door, asking me out of the other Americans' earshot whether she had done something wrong. She then complimented me on my English and began speaking in Russian, trying to settle in her disturbed mind whether I was American or Russian. I responded rather coolly that she had done fine with her answers to the tourists' questions, and that since she liked my English so well, tonight we should speak only in that language. It might help improve hers. She remained befuddled, figuring I *couldn't* be an American, because westerners always had to join these guided groups. If I didn't have a guide, then I would be under the watchful escort of higher Russian officials. What she didn't know was that I had the freedom to travel anywhere, due to my position on the tanker and consequent diplomatic immunity. True, I couldn't go beyond Odessa's city limits, but inside those boundaries I was relatively free.

Upon re-entering the bus, Natasha invited me to sit next to her. But I felt that if I continued to maintain a wall of distance between us, it would make for a more diverting evening. Besides, every American on the bus was now deeply immersed in thought or conversation, also wondering who I was as I strode down the aisle to sit with the duo from Michigan. Within five minutes the bus arrived in front of the Krasny, whereupon Natasha, the mother hen, made another head count to assure herself that all her chicks were safely in tow. As the Americans and the hotel staff carried bags inside, I told Natasha I would be waiting in the lobby while the tourists were assigned rooms, etc. Having come from another Russian city, they were just being settled into the Krasny. Some, I speculated, might have been old Leftists, some successful business people, some braggarts wanting to get home and crow about their trip behind the Iron Curtain. Could they obtain an authentic picture of the country here? Absolutely not. They saw nothing of it at all. Nobody returning to the States could give a proper view of the pre-Gorbachev Soviet Union, because they had no opportunity to meet the common people. The few Russians they talked to all wore western masks.

After a few minutes Natasha came over, asking me if during dinner, I would sit at the head table with her and some local Communist Party dignitaries—medium-ranked officials who were certainly lower on the power scale than types I had met. Again, I declined the opportunity, because I found myself as interested in intriguing them as the Americans, re my identity and purpose here. Let these Soviets view me as some kind of internal security agent, checking current operations. Let them wonder if I was Russian or not. I left the door open for all imaginations, both Soviet and American, to run riot! So I answered Natasha that I'd rather sit with my newfound American friends, adding: "Don't worry, it's going to work out just fine." This patronizing comment created further concern in her mind. Who exactly *was* I?

My greatest joy was to sit with the Americans, watching their faces as they tasted Russian cuisine for which they'd shelled out considerable amounts of cash. I couldn't help chuckling as I watched them saw through the gristle on their plates. Very few complained about the quality of the food, though it was still as bad as ever. There was the usual wine at the table, and that, too, was as poor as it had been three years earlier. Apparently the Russians never obtained a suitable vintage. I looked at the crystal on the table and thought there ought to be a picture here of Jack Casey, the American glass-eating champion. As for the entertainment it was loud and didn't impress me. Luckily, I recognized none of the staff working here from three years earlier. Due to graft and corruption, there was obviously much turnover at the hotel. Jobs like the ones here were constantly sought out by those with power and influence, who could award them to friends or relatives. They were of course considered good positions by allowing Russians to work the black market with near-at-hand western clientele.

Toward the end of the evening, as the party was winding down, Natasha came over and sat next to me. Most everybody—Americans and Russians—had ample amounts of vodka in them, and many of the Soviet officials had already left. A few Americans had also retired for the evening. Natasha seemed determined to get a handle on things, opening up a conversation with me and the other Americans in the vicinity. She wanted to know what part of the States I was from, and with a slightly wicked look of glee, I replied: "Niagara Falls—have you heard of it?" I got a lot of nods from the Americans, and Natasha said it was one of the wonders of the world.

"Are you really from Niagara Falls?" she then asked. To which I retorted: "What makes you think I'm not?" She smiled and said something like: "You know that as an Intourist guide I must go through a lot of training and am responsible for all the tourists—to make sure they are happy. I am sure you understand what a great responsibility that is. I am just surprised," she continued, "that someone like you would emphasize Niagara Falls with our group. Your English is excellent, Comrade." By now the Americans around us were on the edge of their chairs, if they hadn't already fallen off them from the vodka. The upshot is that Natasha wanted to know if I had booked a room at the hotel, or whether I'd be staying in some other location. I explained to her that I had other duties and would soon be leaving; but that I would probably stop back again in the morning. Even the Americans wondered where I was going. With studied hesitancy in my voice, I indicated that a wise traveler *always* has places to stay, ones that no one else needs to know about. The whole ruse provided me much enjoyment. I even told my American friends that I'd drop them a note in the mail, giving further detail on why I had joined them that day—at which Natasha's ears pricked up. She must certainly have thought her job was in peril!

Why had I done all this? Partly to have a good time; but in retrospect I realize that I was also impelled here by a somewhat vindictive spirit. If you want to call me the poor man's Cold Warrior, go ahead. But the whole Soviet situation before *glasnost* and *perestroika* seemed utterly hypocritical to me. In theory they loved Communism, but they also despised it. They loathed capitalism, but seemed to live for its products. Like Lincoln's election speeches on slavery in North and South, these views varied, depending on whether you caught the Russians in public venues, or private ones. Their daily duplicity angered and frustrated me, and I guess I growingly wanted to shine a searchlight on this ideological sham, turning their own system against them.

At evening's end we all shook hands and said goodbye, and I told Natasha I'd keep my eye out for her and that I'd give her superiors a glowing report—to the effect that she was a marvelous comrade. Maybe they would cast a bronzed statue of her, like other brethren around here—in some park or even before a building like the opera house.

The whole charade had been more fun for me than watching pigeons or pacing the streets. I soon left, walking back on empty cobblestoned streets to the ship, at maybe one or two in the morning, but with no threat of danger around.

Thankfully, not all better-off Russians lacked character, and I would receive a rather truthful guide to the Soviet mentality via the afore-mentioned English professor at the University of Odessa, mentor of Intourist guides like Natasha, and the man who gave me that Russian textbook on World War II. His name was Evgeni, or "Lev," and he and his wife Vida became close friends of mine.[11] I met Lev, a Georgian, on one of only two tennis courts in Odessa. The court was lo-

---

[11] The names of husband and wife are pseudonyms.

cated behind the Marisk hotel, and I happened to be there one day, just sitting quietly, watching people rally. That's when Lev arrived, wearing a baseball cap unique to American merchant seamen. It had a very short bill that wouldn't get caught in the wind, and I'd never seen this kind of cap anywhere but on American merchant vessels, particularly in the Gulf Coast area. Curious, I asked where he had acquired it, wondering at first whether he might be working on another American ship; but then I realized that ours was the only one moored in Odessa at the time. The man's English was not so good that it hid his Russian accent, but it was clearly excellent. Lev told me he had bought the cap from a friend who had worked on another American vessel in Russia. I then asked about his English and that's when he told me about his university position.

For the next several weeks I saw Lev and Vida on almost a daily basis. In fact the very day we met, he invited me back to his ground floor apartment to introduce me to his wife. Up till then I'd never set foot in a Russian residence. I was a bit surprised, knowing from a protocol point of view that Russians weren't supposed to converse with westerners, and I questioned Lev about that. He told me the reason he had free access to westerners was because of his demonstrable need to stay abreast of current English usage. He was even permitted to listen openly to Voice of America broadcasts. Despite some distorted viewpoints, including his agreement with that World War II text he gave me, Lev was an interesting person, with a pretty accurate take on American society.

I should add another key reason he and his wife could entertain me virtually on a daily basis: Lev's mother-in-law had been a great war hero. Having glittered in the fight against the Nazis, she was awarded top Soviet honors and a high Communist Party position. Partly due to her influence, Vida also had a rather privileged occupational situation. She was allowed to work at home, reporting weekly to her boss at the university on her translations of scientific publications from English into Russian. Vida spoke very good, Oxfordy English, whereas her hubby sounded like a slangy American, creating a comical contrast. At the time I was there she was working on a scientific report put out by the Woods Hole Oceanographic Institute in New England. I was intrigued by this, asking her and Lev about the quality of the Russian scientific community, and both started to laugh, explaining to me that the reason she was translating these papers was because when done, they were simply stolen, becoming publishing credits for some current Soviet scientist! I can imagine the Russian savant wiping his brow, as though he had actually done the research. But this kind of lying permeated the entire society. Remember the story of why we were bringing grain to the Soviets—because the Russians had supposedly fed America during the war.

Thanks again, at least in part, to mama's reputation, her daughter and son-in-law possessed one of the better living facilities in Odessa, much more comfortable than the average Russian's. They actually had a bathroom in their apartment, and hot and cold running water. It was a two-room flat, with a bedroom/living room containing a fold-out couch, and a kitchen; off the kitchen was a small bath. That kitchen was very small, probably eight by twelve at most, and the living room was about eight by twenty. Yet by Soviet standards they lived well. If, however, you are reading this on a hot summer day, you may wonder about Russian air conditioning. Almost no apartment dwellers in Odessa had it then. My Marisk hotel did, but most of the time it was broken, and it certainly couldn't be relied on. Of course Odessa only got a few really hot days in summer, though the humidity was frequently high.

The average Russian existed in an apartment complex with one hallway bathroom providing toilet and shower. There was also a spigot that came off the wall for filling pots. People took water back to their apartments to boil. (Plumbing was generally not available in the entire building.) Anyway, you'd see people constantly taking these pots and pans into a bathroom serving eight or ten apartments—to get their water. There was a common kitchen, and you had to arrange cooking shifts. Seven families might use one stove, and each had an allotted time period there.

"High rise apartments," one should add, were never over seven or eight stories high in Odessa. After you got above the first floor, walls and ceilings in the corridors were totally out of line. A wall would simply drift in and out, and the whole thing looked as though it had been in a huge earthquake! You could see how the Russians simply painted over and constantly re-plastered cracks, for these places had a most dishevelled look. Add to that a repugnant, musty smell in the buildings, and in corridors 100 feet long, one bulb for light—so dim you couldn't read a paper in it—and this was far from luxury living.

Lev's building was exactly as I've described, and from the second floor up became more and more distorted, due to poor architectural design. There was apparently little skilled labor available, and construction materials were whatever natural material could be found—

nothing synthetic seemed to be around. I could see why even a modest earthquake could devastate cities in this type of society.

Speaking of construction, Soviet buildings were almost never "under construction" but rather, *reconstruction*, since major portions often collapsed. Scaffolding for workers seemed very flimsy; it was often made of rudimentary materials, like bamboo poles!

On the first day I entered Lev's apartment and met Vida, I also met their daughter, Oksana,[12] a tiny pea pod running around with a shirt over her shoulders that only went as far down as her belly button. Maybe twelve or fourteen months old, she was a sweetheart of a little girl. Looking at the diaper situation, and at most everything else here, I began to get a sense of what life must have been like in America of the early 1900s. That was about where the Russian people seemed to be in terms of living standards. Oksana had no diapers and could only have been diapered on rare occasions. In summer especially it was more convenient simply to mop up wherever she decided to discharge. During the course of my time with the family, there were at least two occasions when Oksana sat on my knee and then on handing her back, I found I had a wet leg. If she was scolded by Lev, it wasn't uncommon for her to piddle out of fear.

Like so many in the Soviet Union Lev definitely liked his vodka, and pretty well each night I was there he got half cut. Vida, however, didn't drink much at all. She and I had some very interesting discussions regarding birth control methods. It started with me and Lev, then several days later it became a troika. In his initial conversation on the subject Lev asked if I could get him a few prophylactics from our ship's supply, indicating that the one he possessed was getting worn out! I was shocked to think that he was using the thing over and over; from a hygienic point of view it seemed very risky. So I asked him what he meant by "well-used." He said that after he employed the shield with his wife, they carefully prepared for its use next time. I asked where he had gotten the one he had, and he said "from another ship." He then wanted to know whether he could buy some from me. Within the next day or two I brought about a gross from the ship, so that he could maintain a reasonable supply.

Lev was very happy to receive these items, and a few days after my shipment Vida said during dinner that she too was grateful for what I'd done—bringing Lev the "gifts." She was a bit evasive in her Oxbridge English, but I knew what she meant. Given that she had only one

---

[12] This is a pseudonym.

child, I then asked her a rather bold question on what she had done by way of family planning. The couple were probably already in their late thirties. Vida's face suddenly became red, and tears welled up in her eyes and ran down her cheeks. She became so choked up that she couldn't speak, and momentarily retired to the bathroom. Concerned, I asked Lev if I'd said something out of bounds, and he conveyed to me that items like the pill were an extreme rarity here, and that even when available, many women couldn't take it because it was so chemically powerful that they often experienced terrible side effects. Even those who could had no reliable source of the product. So a more common birth control method here was abortion, especially since Russians frowned on having more than two children per family. This was particularly true in a big city like Odessa, because with a lot of children one became a burden on the rest of society.

When Vida returned, regaining her composure, I apologized to her. She went on to describe with much emotion two abortions she had had before Oksana's birth, and kept repeating how she had killed her son. Tears welled up again, and she seemed truly anguished about disposing of these children. I was grateful for the couple's honesty on this painful subject, though I believed they would also have to report periodically to the secret police about our conversations and my whereabouts. I simply felt that went with the territory.

One evening I departed the ship to go to a restaurant that Lev insisted would provide reasonably good Russian fare. But mostly I brought ashore some of the fine American victuals we had on board, which we then cooked up in their apartment. On many occasions they invited friends over to eat or hang out, and I got to meet a number of Russian couples or single men and women. We had long conversations into the night, where they seemed very open about their views and feelings, though some also became aggressive, attacking me and the American way of life. I guess the Russians couldn't quite get away from the need to rationalize their own poverty. Some seemed happy to confront me about the ruthlessness that obviously was the source of my comparative wealth. In their society "ruthless" and "wealthy" were synonymous. In fact I never flaunted things I had in Russia, though I did bring gifts, for which Lev tried constantly to pay me. On occasion I took his rubles, but prior to sailing away, I would return all this money to him, since it was useless to me.

I remember one time when Lev asked me to accompany him to an afternoon soccer game. He brought along two students, one a Cuban girl who spoke little Russian and even less English, the other a Palestinian Arab. I guess Lev had started his own little U.N., and I think he was intrigued to see what would happen on this occasion, knowing full well that neither Cubans nor Palestinians exactly loved the U.S. I think he was hoping to expose them to a real American, one who would modify their textbook descriptions and clichés. Maybe he wanted them to see that we were all humans, and that we needed to understand each other in order to survive in this unstable world.

The Palestinian, a medical student at Odessa University, berated America—speaking in fairly good English, though Lev had to do some interpreting. We discussed the Middle East, and he obviously hated everything about the Jewish people. His total focus was to return to what he considered Palestinian territory, working in some medical capacity to fight the good fight and help kill off Jews (or Israelis). I don't think my conversation diminished that hateful intensity in him.

The Cuban lady, however, was different, perhaps because she knew America better. For one, she didn't have a religious bone to pick. She was also familiar with baseball, a Cuban passion, and had obviously heard more western music than the Palestinian (conceivably originating from Florida). Too, her parents would have known American culture, having lived in Cuba during the Batista era. She undoubtedly hailed from an elite Party family on her native island, and her purpose in Odessa was to become more educated in Communist philosophy.

I learned as well that there were only a few black Africans at the university here. Lev told me that all Russians called them apemen, considering them to be of simian derivation. They also despised Africans because those they saw were extremely wealthy, with fathers or relatives very high up and close to the dictators who ran their homelands. African blacks frequently came to Russia with a Mercedes and lots of spending money, and the Russian people seethed with jealousy. Despite his putative enlightenment, Lev, too, felt exactly that way about blacks. He had a hard time swallowing the bitter pill that these Africans he saw had more money in their possession than he could amass in a hundred lifetimes (at least in Communist Russia). The Soviets kept their distance from the few blacks who sojourned here, and in fact, they became political untouchables.

One night Lev and I were talking, and as usual he'd had too many drinks, so he opened up about the exodus of Jewish "refuseniks" from Russia in that era. I was surprised to learn that not only were Jews leaving, but many born-again Christians, too. Lev told me that he was secretly engaged in tutoring some of these Jews in English, because they knew that when and if they obtained a visa, it would come in handy, given that the majority would go either to the U.S. or Israel. Lev made a good living on the side teaching these people, though many Russian Jews were losing top jobs for even considering emigration. He further disclosed something interesting about the government's antisemitism. In order to enter university from the secondary school system, high school students had to take entrance exams in several different areas. These examinations were graded by university professors, and Lev told me that when he participated, he was clearly instructed by a political commissar as to which students applying were Jewish. Their test papers received a special designation and Lev was told to make sure these students didn't pass. His job was to find fault with their papers, making them fail in the process. This obviously troubled him, or I doubt he would have mentioned it to me.

More and more, he exposed the hypocritical reality of the Soviet system with which he had to co-exist. One night we were watching television at his place, though I understood very little of what I saw, except the pictures. On the news I happened to see the White House on screen and people holding signs in front of it. When the news story came to an end, Lev starting laughing almost hysterically at what the Russian reporter told his audience. Apparently this reporter described the TV scene as mobs of protesters carrying signs around the White House, showing how an oppressive capitalist society was undermining the will of the American people. The Americans had no political freedom because everything there was owned by only a few people. The reporter had gone on to note that unlike in the Soviet Union, where all were comrades and shared equally, this demonstration revealed how the American masses still needed to procure their fair share of the pie. Lev knew that Americans at least *had* the freedom to protest. If anyone ever made a sign and carried it in Communist Russia, denouncing government policies, they'd be imprisoned for years. Between the lines, Lev seemed to be implying that freedom should be highly cherished, and that it might be more important to life than physical sustenance or material comforts.

For even Lev and Vida had to endure some of the same strictures as ordinary Russians. For example, all Soviet men and women had to work, and when a mother had a child, she typically received only six months of child care time. After that the child was essentially turned over to a state agency to be raised during the day. When mothers were on the job, all Russian children were brought up in these state-run daycare centers. At that time this seemed truly scary, but today, with two-career families the norm, America has basically gone the same route of stripping kids from parents. Breaking up the family can obviously intensify a society's anarchic tendencies, but over there, young people at least had iron fists near at hand. Transgressing against laws in the Soviet Union brought no mercy.

If, however, you simply became a drunk out of frustration, the law could care less. Most Russian males, including Lev, seemed to be serious alcoholics, partly because they had lost that vital human commodity, hope.

The booze he relentlessly drank each night certainly helped my professor friend loosen his tongue about these societal problems. He was clearly distraught about the dilemma in which he found himself—his heart and mind striving to be free, but his professional situation demanding he kowtow to political realities in an oppressive society. One evening he and his wife and I went to a restaurant, and having quaffed a couple drinks at the flat beforehand, Lev was pretty far gone by the end of the meal. The more he drank, the more he spoke openly about his heartfelt desires, directly condemning the Russian government for their policies and system.

Leaving the restaurant, we embarked on about a two-mile walk back to the apartment. Like most Soviet citizens, Lev didn't own a car. If average Russians tried to acquire such a luxury, it would demand a good ten years savings, and as a result they'd live in even worse poverty. As we walked the darkened streets, I suddenly noticed Vida's face turn white in the midst of our conversation. Grabbing Lev by the arm, she said something in Russian, and pulling him ahead, both then ran, with Lev hollering at me to "stay back, stay back!" I was somewhat confused by these actions, wondering whether I had offended them. I knew something must be going on here. Following at a distance, and not sure whether to head for their apartment or the ship, I saw the couple disappear into an underground subway. I then went down, too, finding a path lit by only a few bulbs and some very dark alcoves. At the bottom of the stairs I didn't see Lev and Vida, so I walked over to what I presumed was the exit. Then I heard a noise emanating from one of the darkened alcoves—a kind of "psst." There was Lev's eerie silhouette, and him motioning me to get in there quick. I ran over and he rapidly warned me with finger on his lips to be quiet. I stood there, watching the lit path area I'd just left, and then two plain-clothed Russian security agents walked down the corridor I'd hastily vacated. My greatest concern was not for my own safety—I knew I was untouchable here—but for my friends. I guess Lev had lulled me by reassuring me that he was always secure, due to his special need for English practice.

After a few minutes we vacated the dark alcove, went back the way we had come in, and left the Russian agents going in the other direction. In tears Vida spoke rapidly to Lev, and we took a different route back to their apartment. Once in the door Lev explained Vida's nearly hysterical reaction in the street. She was concerned that one of the men following them was a very powerful government agent whom she knew through her mother. For him to follow them was not a good sign. Lev then downed a few more drinks and rather loudly, started to curse out the first floor window. Vida tried to quieten him down, and I pulled Lev from the window sill and at the same time, noticed bodies stir in the shrubbery below. Apparently the agents had determined they would listen to our conversation from this vantage point. Lev was too loaded to be truly attentive to the situation, so I backed him into the middle of the room and motioned him and his wife into the bathroom, out of earshot of eavesdroppers. I explained that two men were under the window sill and obviously wished to hear our conversations. At that point Vida broke down and cried, and between sobs, kept mumbling something to Lev. He then explained to me that he and his wife had to report on a weekly basis to the secret police, giving them a full account of their whereabouts as well as mine. I felt this problem tonight related to that assignment. Lev confessed that from the beginning his mission had been to report to them on my activities in Russia. He told me that these orders had come down from Captain Bazarov, who he also felt had instigated a special security watch on us tonight.

A few minutes later, however, Vida regained some poise, obviously assessing the situation and concluding that her mother's high position *was*, in fact, unassailable. Impulsively she now went into the kitchen and filling up a pot with water, took it to the window and poured it out onto the watchers. This elicited a lot of noise and commotion, then an inebriated Lev climbed up on the sill, announcing his intention to urinate down below! Vida half restrained him, but we all started laughing with relief. Up till then I had been very concerned, but I now realized that they must have made a decision that the whole thing was less dangerous than it had first appeared.

The next day Vida went to see her mother, telling her what had occurred the night before. Through a chain of command her mother promptly instructed the local security goons to call off their surveillance of her daughter and son-in-law. Before that Vida's mother hadn't been aware of the problem. As I have said, Soviet war heroes carried plenty of clout, frequently walking the streets wearing medals. Even though elderly, they were highly respected by the common people, as well as feared, because they often had powerful positions.

The constant parade of friends coming to Lev's and Vida's continued, due to the presence of an American sea captain there. Even though the equivalent of upper middle class in Russia, Lev and Vida had no telephone in their flat to use for invitations, and this was pre-email; so one had to communicate with people more directly. In fact, there were no telephones in the entire building, which was apparently typical for Odessa. Generally there were payphones on street corners, so people would call at certain times to those who lived across the city, and the call would be received at another payphone. More often people simply stopped by.

A flood of individuals came over, and I asked Lev whether that was common—seeing five or six people at minimum visit in a typical evening. He admitted that it was a combination of both the phone shortage and Lance Orton's presence there. Lev told me that Vida had put the word out about me. So people dropped over, intrigued to see what I looked and acted like, and that reflected well on his wife. In a putatively egalitarian society the Russians were constantly vying for position and power, which could also include looking for ways to inflict blackmail—i.e., via the threat of denunciation to the secret police. However, in Vida's and Lev's home most guests talked quite freely. Of course few spoke English with even moderate facility, so Lev kept helping them out.

One woman, in particular, seemed to be visiting more and more steadily, and it got to the point where she was there virtually every time I was. This Svetlana, a blond lady, spoke only a little English, always requiring interpretive help. Yet she invariably hung around for a couple hours. How to describe her? I guess you would call her good-looking, but in common with most Russians, she had poor teeth. Even Vida, a beauty, made you cringe when she opened her mouth. I should add that personal hygiene was also not up to the American standard, understandably so, for they just didn't have the amenities. Their lack of underarm deodorant could certainly be perceived. Bathing was of course difficult, for an apartment complex might contain but one shower for the entire building, located by a toilet constantly in use. Many resorted to lugging pots and pans of water into their flats to try and get clean.

Back to Svetlana's many visits. Whenever she came over, I noticed that she and Vida first chatted in another room for five minutes or so, punctuated by a lot of giggling; then they would come in to where Lev and I were talking. For a few minutes Vida then tried to strike up a rather artificial conversation with us, and eventually we would get back to normal. But Svetlana always stayed her two hours or so.

Finally one evening, waiting till Svetlana had departed, I asked Vida about the frequency of her visits. I wondered whether she was Vida's best friend, but she shrugged and said "not really." Unwilling to discuss it further, Vida instead conferred in Russian with her husband. Then she went into the kitchen, letting Lev answer my query. He smiled and said: "Svetlana's interested in you, Lance, and would do anything that you wanted." I laughed a little and responded: "What does she think she'd gain by this? There are plenty of Russian men around here who at least speak the language." Vida was listening in the other room and again spoke loudly in Russian, and Lev started laughing, and I asked for a translation. He said that according to Vida, "few Russian women would turn down an American sea captain. When they are grandmothers, they will be able to tell their grandchildren this fine story." I found all that highly amusing, and we continued laughing a while, though I'm sure that I also turned a little red.

Finally I collected myself, saying: "Vida, I hope you've made it clear to these people that I'm married and have certain standards I live by." In fact we had already had a number of interesting conversations about Christianity and its principles. Of course neither Lev nor Vida were Christians; almost certainly they were atheists. However, by the time I finally left for the States, I think they respected my views enough to wonder whether there might indeed be a God up there.

Nothing could induce me to get any closer to Svetlana, though the whole thing gave me another interesting take on the amoral condition of Soviet society. Russian marriages didn't seem founded on moral principles at all. And it turned out that Svetlana was herself married to a chief officer who must often be away on a Russian merchant ship. She may have been a spy or just lonely, or both.

But all this made me comprehend why the Russian divorce rate was so high. Surprisingly, that didn't seem to bother Soviet authorities, so repressive in other domains. Russian divorces in that era must have been at least as rife or more so than ours. Alcoholism obviously played its role, and so did the fact of having children taken away from their parents all day long.

Soviet hypocrisy and inconsistencies kept assaulting me, and I continued to play games with them. Poor Boris, my obsequious chauffeur, became another victim. It started one day when I was leaving the ship, with its usual contingent of Red Army soldiers guarding the vessel from unauthorized civilians wishing to board. Usually six to eight Russian soldiers surveyed the ship and each other, too, because a soldier might also consider defecting. These men were locked and loaded at all times—ready to fire even on each other.

So here I was, leaving the ship and reaching the bottom of the gangway, when a Russian soldier brought up his rifle from his side to a cross-chest position in order to make me stop. The man was obviously a new recruit because I didn't recognize him. In a curt command he told me to "Stop!" and I walked around him, and again he shouted "Stop!" I turned toward him, and with bayoneted rifle he pointed at my briefcase. "Stop!" he shouted a third time. I put down my briefcase right beside him, and in deliberate English told him: "Call Captain Bazarov—now." And then I added: "I'm the captain." He pointed again at the briefcase, which of course I kept with me at all times when going ashore, since it contained important security items like sliced cheese and popcorn seeds for Lev, Vida, and their friends. (They had never had popcorn before my arrival.) Anyway, I retreated to where I had deposited the briefcase, picked it up, and started to walk down to the dock.

Meanwhile, Boris had been watching all this intently. His position in the secret police working directly under Bazarov would be well known to Red Army soldiers here. Suddenly he shouted loudly at the Russian guard—his voice resonating between the hull of the ship and the shanty steel dock warehouses. In a quick double step, the guard ran past me down the dock. To me he resembled a poor dog whistled in by its owner, and when he reached Boris, he stopped abruptly and saluted. Though a rather shabbily dressed man in civilian clothes, Boris was able to reprimand this man in no uncertain terms.

As I ambled over to the scene, my chauffeur then offered me his hand in apology, implying that this would never happen again. To which the Russian soldier nodded his head in abject agreement. After another of Boris' quick orders in Russian, the humiliated guard ran back in double time to his original position.

Now to this point I'd been told by Bazarov that Boris couldn't speak English. My usual custom was to get into his car and point out on a map where I wanted to go, more or less the same route through Odessa's streets each time, with my habitual destination the Marisk. I always figured that the chauffeur could, in fact, speak English and I was determined to find out. And today, good fortune happily came to the rescue. Halfway through the city on our usual route, we arrived at an intersection uncommonly stopped up with vehicles (given that Russia had so few cars, this construction delay was unusual).

On this day I actually had a bona fide appointment at the hotel with the Russian steamship agent, followed by a special club event that night. So I became frustrated by the delay at the construction site, knowing that I'd be late for my meeting. We sat there for about ten minutes, then I abruptly opened up the car door and jumped out. When I did, Boris started hollering in Russian, whereupon I smiled briefly, slammed the door, and took off down this cobble-stoned street. When I got to the first alley, I darted toward it, knowing the problems I was creating for Boris, still stuck in that traffic jam. The poor chauffeur had never seen me do this before. His job was to know my whereabouts. Whenever he drove me to the hotel, he would remain in the car outside the building, until I informed him that for the rest of the day I would use my feet, and no longer needed him. I'd simply wave him off and say "nyet," before my usual walk to Lev's and Vida's. But today's action was highly unusual: what would he report back to Bazarov? Boris must have been sweating profusely, figuring I had some very important, clandestine meeting to make.

As I ran down the alley, much to my surprise I heard footsteps and turned around—Boris in hot pursuit! He had obviously left his car standing in the traffic, racing behind me to learn where I was going. Probably in his early fifties and overweight, he hollered at me in Russian, and I hollered back that I didn't speak that language. I kept on running, lengthening the distance between us. In total exasperation Boris finally shouted in English: "Stop Captain Orton! Please stop.... I'll lose my job. Stop!"

I knew that if Russian government personnel could even superficially get through their daily tasks, they would generally come out unscathed. But an event like this one might have potentially dangerous consequences for him. After Boris had blown his "no English" cover, I abruptly halted, turned around, and saw him in a position that seemed like a heart attack in process, chest heaving, head cocked upward, panic scribbled all over his face.

I now hollered back: "Boris, your English is excellent. Congratulations!" Then I took off again, continuing on my way. Boris gave up his pursuit and I arrived on foot at the Marisk for my meeting.

A few days later I ran into Bazarov, with whom I had already had verbal duels over ship's operations, charter obligations, or simply the capitalist versus the Communist system. We were natural, round-the-clock adversaries. It was like a constant chess game, and the Russians certainly loved their chess. Odessa had a lot of parks, and every day you would see older people playing or watching it there. TV hadn't made the same seductive inroads in Russia as it had in the States—filled with Big Brother propaganda, it didn't command much attention. So chess was very popular.

Anyhow, Bazarov, the human chess player, talked to me about Boris's problem the day of the traffic jam, and I simply smiled, saying: "Dimitri, I'm surprised at what a quick study your driver was. For a while we'd had a language problem, but suddenly he was speaking almost perfect English. I can see that I've been a good influence on him, and now that he knows English, you can use him anywhere." Then I lowered my voice and added: "You don't suppose that Boris knew English all along?" With a grin my adversary replied: "No, not our Boris." I then said I hadn't seen the chauffeur for several days since the street decathalon and hoped he wasn't in hospital. Bazarov said the chauffeur was simply taking a little vacation. I smiled, telling Dimitri I hoped the vacation was in Odessa, not Siberia. With a chuckle Bazarov said that Boris would be back next week, and indeed, he was.

From then on my chauffeur would proffer a few words in English each time we met. The first thing I asked him on his return to work was whether he might like a pair of western sneakers. He laughed as hard as I've ever seen a Russian laugh, and after about two minutes said quietly in English: "I hope everything went well that night." I suddenly realized that all this was a big game to these people! Boris didn't really care to know what had happened that evening; all he cared about was not getting caught off base himself.

Selecting a pair of sneakers on the ship that would fit him, I asked Bazarov's permission to give them to Boris as a gift. Bazarov surely considered me a smart ass, which was fine by me, for I enjoyed putting sticks in the wheels of their system.

The particular day and night Boris had been so worried about included my visit to the Peruse (or Sail) Club, which I'll now describe. At the Marisk I'd met with one of the Russian agents from Inflot, the government agency with jurisdiction over all Soviet maritime affairs. They acted as liaisons between foreign ships and the Russian government to comply with Soviet law. As well, they helped expedite the ship's stay in port—supervising communication with longshoremen, or offering any other assistance a ship's captain might need. The difficulty here stemmed from the great difference between the West and the Soviet Union. In the West steamship agents acted on behalf of the company, by whom they were paid. They would consequently do all they could to help a ship complete its operations, assisting the captain in any way he considered appropriate. If he needed $50,000 in cash, he simply told the steamship agent to make arrangements with the home office and have it sent. If he needed special documents for port clearance or departure, the agent contacted the requisite departments and procured the documents. If he had personnel joining or departing the ship, and wanted a steamship agent to pick them up at the airport or escort them to a police station, the person handled that, too. Agents were a great aid, and being paid by the company, had to perform to a certain standard.

But pre-Gorbachev Russia ran under a very different system. The first priority of steamship agents assigned by Inflot to a visiting ship was to preserve themselves from anything that might imperil their position, or those of their government employers. I always found it comical to watch these agents play the part of my allies, when in fact, they were adversaries. More than once I laughed out loud in front of them, as they tried to resolve a problem in my behalf with some other government official.

In other words if you had a fire out of control, and this guy's supposed to be part of the fire fighting crew, the best you could hope for was that he'd be an observer to that fire. More often, however, these Soviet agents simply threw gasoline on the blaze!

The steamship agent I met that day at the Marisk was very close to my age and obviously hoped to establish a friendly relationship with me. He was openly, palpably shallow and had more strings attached to him than Howdy-Doody. Always anxious about losing his job, he couldn't focus on any shipboard problem I might have. Instead, he was looking out solely for number one and thinking of how to enhance his power, which he truly enjoyed exercising.

One day at my captain's table, where this Yuri was wolfing down huge quantities of American food, I asked if he was enjoying his lunch, and he replied in a quasi-surly way that he was, but that Russian food was equally delicious. I grinned, asking if there was any place in Odessa, besides our ship, that could provide a decent meal. Sitting near us were seven or eight Soviet port officials, who mostly couldn't speak English, but who also knew how to fill their faces. I commented to Yuri that if there was good food available in Odessa, it was odd to see our wardroom filled each day with Russian officials eating so heartily here. That's when he suggested that I rendezvous with him one day after work at the Marisk; from there he would take me to a gastronomic wonderland called the Peruse Club.

       TURBULENT SEAS

My arrival on foot at the Marisk caught Yuri by surprise, because he was fully aware of my constant driver escort. But I pressured him to move our schedule along so that we could arrive at the Peruse before dark, which he did. The club was situated on a high bluff overlooking the Black Sea. From there downward was a lot of underbrush and trails people used to get to the water. The club was by no means extravagant in appearance. It was in a very casual, open-air, cement building, obviously intended only as a summer operation. A good portion of the building had no windows, and there was no way to enclose the edifice for a long Russian winter. Lights strung along the patio made the Peruse look somewhat Christmasy, but it was not unlike a beachside American club.

On entering, you found the place opened up immediately to an area where there were twenty-five or thirty tables jammed close together—so close that you'd be careful backing your chair up, in order to avoid bumping someone. Every table in here was full. People were also standing by a bar, and the crowd spilled onto an adjoining patio area, filled with young offspring of the Russian elite class. In the main these were probably sons and daughters of World War II veterans— Russian baby boomers clad in the finest of blue jeans, or tee-shirts bearing lettering that again might challenge their understanding, but which seemed de rigueur to wear. Despite this western garb the majority here couldn't seem to speak English.

Music playing when we arrived was some kind of Russian folk song blaring loudly, but within a minute or two, the Beatles replaced it on the speakers. Yuri walked us to one of the tables in the room, abruptly negotiating the departure of folks already sitting there. They moved out to the patio and he invited me to take a seat. Within minutes he was talking to people at neighboring tables, and soon the other four chairs at ours were filled with women, laughing and checking out my attire, and wondering how they might communicate with me. The waiter came over, putting two full bottles of poor Russian wine and one of vodka on our table. Yuri and the women attacked the liquor with obvious zest. I could see that he was at the center here, hugely basking in the glow of his own importance. He asked me to tell one of the women about my background and translated into Russian—that I was captain of the largest ship ever moored in Odessa, and so on. They all kind of oohed and aahed, and by that time people here seemed to perceive me and Yuri as celebrities. I didn't comprehend what was being said, but Yuri was basically patting himself on the back, letting people know he was with a VIP. Of course I did have diplomatic immunity, and few had seen an American of that status freed from the Intourist leash. However, being gawked at as though I were a creature in a zoo made me increasingly uncomfortable.

At one point a soused Russian came to our table, exhaling foul, tooth-decayed breath. He would have been no more than thirty or so, yet when he approached me with something important to say, he almost knocked me off my chair. Yuri stood up and apparently ordered him back to his table. It turned out that there was an argument over which western group was singing the song on the sound system. The argument was basically between Foul-Mouthed Eddie and his girlfriend. Because the Russians considered me an automatic expert on western music, my answer would settle the matter. One thought the group was the Beatles, the other something like the Dave Clark Five, and I wasn't sure who was right. I asked which side Eddie took, and which position the girl espoused. I figured I'd side with the lady because I felt sorry for her having to endure an evening of that fellow's exhalations. Whatever she was going to gain via a bet was fine with me. So my less than expert testimony decided the dispute.

Speaking of teeth, I should probably add that toothbrushes were rare items in the Soviet Union. If they even had one, people usually used a stick split at different angles with a bunch of twiggy endings, which they would then scrape across their teeth. I'm not sure if you could find bona fide toothbrushes at the grocery stores—I certainly never saw any. Vida and Lev were amazed when I brought them real ones. At first Vida thought I was giving her the smallest scrub brush she'd ever seen. The care of teeth couldn't have been a high priority there.

Anyhow, with my judging done, everyone seemed to focus even more strongly on us, as though we were the hub in a wheel, and people at other tables the spokes. But to my surprise they soon switched off the music, and suddenly everybody yanked bottles off the table, putting them at their feet. There was a lot of nervous hush and commotion in the room, and it looked as though people here were trying to clean up their acts in a great hurry. I asked Yuri about this sudden transformation, and he answered: "Police are coming." I asked him why we weren't putting our bottles on the ground, too, but he replied: "Don't worry, no problem for you, Lance." I felt that Yuri was looking to escalate his power base in front of all these high-class people, using me as part of his repertoire; so I told him firmly to put the bottles on the ground like everyone else.

As the cops strode into the room, I thought of the Gestapo in Occupied Europe during World War II, searching cafés for resistants. These two policemen swaggered from table to table, checking faces and obviously sending cold chills down the backs of patrons. The atmosphere had become deathly silent. Everyone had vacated the bar, and some of the Soviet gilded youth had left by a back exit. No one spoke. One of the policemen came over and scrutinized my face, and I asked Yuri: "Has this guy got a problem with me?" The cop then grabbed one of our bottles, and as he started lifting it, Yuri shouted at him in Russian—"Take your hands off!" or something like that. The policeman stared, and when the other one came over from another table, he said something to him in Russian. Yuri identified himself and me too, and both cops came unravelled. Yuri then put the spurs to them, informing them that if they wanted to keep their jobs, they'd better offer me a sincere apology, because they had just messed with an important westerner, one who didn't want trouble from the locals tonight. Both policemen looked sheepishly at me, and with open hands and palms gesturing, they uttered something in Russian that was presumably an apology; then they left quickly by the same door where they had entered. Before they could get out, the crowd renewed its former conversational pitch, and several in the room—apparently drunk—openly cursed the cops behind their backs, sitting down quickly enough so that they couldn't be identified.

Western rock came back on again, and the party continued with obvious relief in the air, because these police officers were greatly feared. I think patrons now realized they wouldn't be bothered the rest of the evening. I asked Yuri if he had enjoyed the opportunity of exercising his power against the police, and he said: "Yes, of course." Being rather young, he obviously ignored the fact that the power he wielded could one day be turned against himself, and that if the system broke down, he'd have a lot of people who hated him.

The scrumptious food I had been longing to sample was now delivered to our table–an entree of chicken pot pie. But you'd have done better ordering this item in any school cafeteria back in the States. The Odessan version had a thick, hard, shelled crust, and one needed something like a chisel to bang it open. Thankfully the spoon provided us was made of heavy gauge iron, which I succeeded in driving through that cement exterior, using half my body weight to do the job. Bottles gyrated on the table as I broke open the crust, and out of the aperture I had made oozed this yellowish substance. I took a few sniffs of that glorious chicken pie, figuring it might have been concocted from the amputated leg of some poor fellow! For it smelled downright awful. While gulping down his portion, and letting gravy run liberally down his chin, Yuri urged me to taste this local specialty. I knew people were watching, so I carefully lifted my spoon, looked around, took a bite, and using all my willpower, kept from spitting it back on the table, managing to swallow a bite of this supposed delicacy. Yuri meanwhile had finished his, so I happily pushed the rest of my pie across the table, watching him finish that one as well—and in record time.

The women kept laughing and by this point, seemed to understand that I was anything but amused by Yuri, and that I would not be used by him. One of the gals also kept trying to touch my hand. Each time mine rested on the table, she edged hers over. Babbling in Russian, she used any pretext to do so. I simply nodded and smiled, but kept myself away from her.

Yuri would not stop being self-important, until I curtly informed him that I was leaving. Hurt, he asked me why, and I said I didn't like some two-bit opportunist using me like a trained bear. I told him that whether he stayed or not was immaterial to me; *I* was leaving. It was about a one-and-a-half mile walk back to the Marisk.

Pondering a bit, Yuri decided to leave with me, and as we pushed through the crowd, everyone in the place was hollering to get our attention. I told Yuri that the next day I would ask Inflot to provide me a new steamship agent. The following morning I indeed notified Bazarov, and after arguing for several minutes, the KGB boss agreed to assign a different official to my ship. I never saw Yuri again, which caused me no sorrow. Without question he was a rising star in the Communist Party, knowing how to intimidate people and wield his power.

The same methods, but with more polish and sophistication, had certainly worked for Bazarov himself. Completely responsible for all KGB operations in the Southern Ukraine—not only in the big port of Odessa, but Sebastopol and other port areas—this suave Dimitri had positioned himself well in the Soviet Merchant Marine to attain a high position. As a young officer he had risen rapidly to become captain of a bulk carrier at a comparatively early age. He must have done well with shipboard commissars in order to ascend the KGB's ladder. Bazarov was a natty dresser, fond of western suits and especially, of fine shoes. In his early fifties he was handsome and distinguished, and had even benefited from western-style dental work. Of course Merchant Marine people were already upper echelon, getting autos and liberties that ordinary Russians couldn't dream of having. They got to see the rest of the world, and bring back lots of nice things for themselves and their families, part of the buy-off to keep them from possible defection. Ironically, merchant mariners in the States were often perceived as the dregs of society, including a goodly number of alcoholics. In our country the trade somehow attracted dysfunctional, if often interesting individuals who had to be confined to floating jails in order to arrive on time for work. As seen, on American ships I frequently found myself performing several capacities at once—among them, psychiatrist, sheriff, and prison guard!

Even in Russia some of my crew managed to find trouble shortly after our arrival. Local officials had cleared the port for limited visitation, whereby our men, if free from duties, might go ashore between nine a.m. and five p.m. They had a strict curfew, instituted by the Soviet government, and had to be back no later than five. The same curfew obtained for all shipboard personnel on virtually all other western ships. (Of course it was different for a captain.)

One result of these daytime leaves was that local women of the night had to do brisk business while the sun shone. There were usually foreign ships in port, and these gals would service a variety of nationalities.

One day several of our crew members decided to go ashore together, heading straight for one of the local hotels where Russian prostitutes gathered. Apparently there was a bar and entertainment area there where the women met the men. They would chat, then take clients back to their flats or other private locations. This hotel area was one of the designated spots in Odessa where it was safe for prostitutes to ply their trade. Local police wouldn't harass them there, but in good '20s Chicago style, one certainly had to pay them off. Russian authorities also used these women to watch for any espionage, a big joke to me—I mean that my whore hounds would bother to spy on the side! Cops also blackmailed these ladies into getting them nice gifts from the customers—blue jeans and other western wares. The women all had full-time, government-assigned jobs, many in nursing, maintaining the politically correct fiction that there was no prostitution in the Soviet Union; but to absent themselves from work, they had to pay off their bosses, too. In theory they were always at work, in practice never. Theirs was certainly an expensive business in Russia, because of all the people on the take.

So our guys went ashore to this hotel bar, and on arrival, apparently found the women entertaining another bunch from a Filipino ship. As soon as the Americans entered, the Russian women dropped their Filipinos like they had the plague, for MONEY had obviously walked in the door. Not only was currency a big object, and items like jeans or razor blades; but the biggest pot of gold that the odd Russian whore might get was a free ticket back to America. Perhaps it took a good actress to swing it, but there were cases of such women beguiling these idiots into thinking they had found potential wives. A guy would end up getting engaged, going through all sorts of turmoil and paperwork to take a future spouse to the U.S. Once having become an American citizen, the gal would then drop him quickly. To the prostitutes it was all money-driven. In fact they may well have noticed the wealth of the West before many other Russians did.

The Filipinos obviously didn't enjoy sudden rejection, and apparently their tempers boiled over. Feeling shortchanged, they thought they would make an issue of it. My silly American crewmen wouldn't back down either, so a fight broke out. It was a typical bar brawl, where tables went one way and chairs another, fists flew, objects were thrown, knives were pulled, and the women exited stage right, while the men tried forcibly to settle who should have them. Local police soon arrived and got into the tussle themselves, and the end result was that some of my crew members had their butts good and kicked. Some were missing teeth, while others had broken hands and fingers, busted ribs, or superficial knife wounds, requiring trips to the hospital.

The way I learned about this fight was by an urgent radio message to the ship from a crew member involved, asking me to come ashore as soon as possible. Several of the crew were now lying bleeding and untreated in the shipping offices across from our vessel, which housed Soviet officials, including Bazarov. I promptly ordered a shoreside launch to come to the ship and bring me there for my personal investigation. On shore I beheld these injured fellows strewn on the cold flagstones of the building's first floor, moaning and crying. Demanding immediate medical treatment for their injuries, I also wanted the chief of police to report to me on what had taken place. I further demanded that the perpetrators be immediately apprehended and arrested. At that point I still wasn't clear that the brawl had involved another ship's crew. I thought our guys might simply have run amok with some of the local population. As I could have predicted, they obviously hadn't hung together, lacking loyalty to each other; so I felt no pity for them. My bigger concern was covering myself legally. By law I had to take immediate action to secure owners of the vessel and myself from criticism. I could even be brought up on charges in the States for failing to fulfill protective obligations toward Americans under my supervision.

According to U.S. law, the master of a vessel must try to the best of his ability to bring his people back safely to American soil.

After getting the real story, I realized this had been a scrap between two crews, and that local authorities probably couldn't do much here. When the police chief arrived, I nonetheless interrogated him through an interpreter (the steamship agent) as to why my crew members would be subjected to this kind of attack on Soviet soil. Demanding a complete report within twenty-four hours, I threatened that I might otherwise have to inform our embassy in Moscow that Americans had been assaulted in Russia. (By this time all my maimed puppies were at the hospital, with the ship's second officer dispatched to watch over them.)

Odessa's police chief had obviously rushed down here—extremely concerned when I hinted that the American Embassy in Moscow might be notified. He quickly got on the phone, and within fifteen minutes, Bazarov had also arrived, showing his own concern about letting such information reach a wider audience. He said that after I had checked on my men in the hospital, he wanted me to stop back in here. Along with the police chief he would convene an immediate inquiry with any pertinent authorities, Soviet citizens, or perpetrators who had been involved.

Soviet hospitals were a sight to see, as long as you weren't stuck in one! Boris drove me over and dropped me off, and I marveled at what I beheld inside. If America is concerned about the quality of its health care, it should compare that quality to what the Soviets had to endure. First off, their hospitals had no private or even semi-private rooms. All they had were wards, undifferentiated by specialities. In other words, people with infectious diseases and broken legs might lie in the same area. Wards contained twenty or thirty beds, and sheets and linens were gray, gnarly, and unpressed. It seemed like they hadn't been washed in months. The only air in the hospital came in through unscreened open windows. So while patients were recuperating, the flies received free meals! This might have been a hospital for humans, but for those flies it was a round-the-clock cafeteria.

By the time I arrived, my crew members' injuries were bandaged up and pretty much taken care of, and hospital attendants informed me that several would have to stay here a number of days, until they had healed. I was amazed to hear most of these guys begging to return to the ship! But I had no intention of making things easy for them, and it would also be difficult for a non-physician to justify their removal from medical care. I thought it a good idea to let them recuperate in these wretched conditions. Maybe it would drum some common sense into their skulls. I also knew that it would protect me from second-guessing back home, emanating from those who didn't really know the Soviet Union. Remembering the legal beagles on my heels when I had been a third officer, I felt I should remain vigilant.

After checking to see that my injured had been treated, I returned to the port facility for the inquiry. The meeting included the police chief, Captain Bazarov, and some of the local police and officials, about fifteen people in all, including a Filipino in his mid-fifties. By this time I'd heard the yowlings of my crew, to the effect that they had been bushwhacked by at least several thousand men!

Using the steamship agent as interpreter, I was given an opportunity to start the interrogation. Bazarov invited me to ask any questions regarding the incident, and I started by explaining that under American law I needed answers as to why my crew members were lying in hospital. If I didn't get them, this incident could escalate into a potential powder keg between two superpowers. I showed I wasn't about to back down, and I could see that Bazarov feared this. Getting quickly to the heart of the matter, I asked where the incident had taken place. I interrogated the police chief and the Oriental fellow, introduced as the captain of another ship moored in the port of Odessa. The latter told me that his crew had been ashore in the hotel bar mentioned, and he was here to defend them from any Soviet repercussions or constraints placed on his ship or crew members. He admitted that several of his men had come back talking about some fight, and I asked whether they had sustained any injuries. He said no, none seemed bothered enough to miss work. This made me chuckle, thinking of my macho ducks recuperating in that awful Soviet hospital. These were the same guys who on the way to Russia had already revealed themselves as intermittent slackers.

My crew's character flaws notwithstanding, I wasn't about to let local Soviet officials off the hook regarding the incident. I hoped to manipulate them and use borderline blackmail tactics, knowing there would be other occasions when I'd have to employ the edge I obtained here to get certain shipboard efficiencies, maintain proper loading schedules, and so forth. In other words I wanted to use the bar incident to procure some leverage.

Rather heatedly, I berated local police officials, asking why they hadn't responded sooner to the incident, hoping to scare them into cooperation down the road. In western culture this strategy would have backfired, because all you would get was undying antipathy from the other side. But in Soviet Russia everything was who you knew and what power you could wield. The power I had behind me was the American government. I emphasized that nothing like this must recur, and they seemed to understand, hoping the matter wouldn't go any further.

Bazarov finally said: "Captain Orton, I fear that you may want to be on the cover of *Time Magazine* from all this!" (I knew he was an avid reader of American journalism.) My response was simply this: "If that's what it takes to protect my crew from members of foreign vessels or local people, I'll do it." I reiterated that "your authorities are responsible for maintaining civil order in areas near where my ship operates." The meeting then ended and I got what I'd hoped for. After a brief discussion in Russian, Bazarov and the police chief announced that to protect American crew members involved in the altercation, perhaps their shore privileges ought to be rescinded. I considered this a fine idea, because now I wouldn't have to be their babysitter!

Returning to Bazarov himself, it became ever more apparent to me that the man had one foot in Russia and another in the U.S. As seen, great Soviet bulk carriers, like the ones he had plied, traveled frequently to the States, and especially to the Mississippi River area, where there were many grain elevators for the loading of foodstuffs from our heartland. These Soviet vessels, like ours, were serviced by American chandlers, supplying ships with products ranging from sundries to heavy machinery and equipment, paint and navigation charts— almost like a general store for the maritime industry.

One ship chandler in Baton Rouge, it turned out, had made good money off his business with Soviet ships. He and his wife were fluent in Russian, and I would find out that they took private vacations in the Soviet Union. Through the influence of eminent KGB like Bazarov, they were not required to travel with an Intourist chaperone watching over them.

I learned all this one night when Bazarov organized a party on my behalf—to take place a story above the first-floor port offices where we had our post-brawl meeting. This was evidently a central KGB location. Bazarov was still perplexed by me, suspecting that my age was unusual for American sea captains, given that the majority were in their late forties at the youngest, and usually late fifties. Perhaps like Khrushchev with the newly-elected Kennedy, he simply wanted to test my comparative youth. In any event his interest in me seemed inordinately high. Arranging this special party in my honor, and always making a car and driver available to me, indicated possible concern about ulterior missions I might have while in Russia.

The way I got invited to the bash was that one night when I returned to the ship about 11:30 p.m. from Lev's and Vida's, and re-entered the port area, security people passed me a note from Bazarov. It said that he had arranged a soirée for all the local dignitaries, as well as various captains and their wives (mostly foreign merchant mariners). The party would honor the arrival and cargo operations of the *Golden Endeavor* (though we'd been here at least a month). Bazarov knew that he hadn't yet gotten a handle on me or my activities. He had perhaps originally felt that I might befriend him, but I hadn't gone for that. My previous Russian experience told me how such socialization could result in ships' officers compromising their ability to act in the company's best interests. Like anyone who reached the top in Soviet Russia, Bazarov was a master at taking advantage of character weaknesses. Not having located mine, he'd obviously decided to give it one more try and throw this party. He certainly had a good pretext, for ours was the largest ship ever seen in Odessa, and intriguing to other captains as well. Perhaps our relative paucity of numbers contributed too, for the size of the American Merchant Marine had dwindled to the point where some other countries now had larger fleets plying the world's trade. I guess there was also that curiosity about my age as a captain. So Bazarov could draw a pretty good crowd. His plan would obviously be to goad me into a personal conversation, gaining insights into my true nature.

After reading the invitation, I sent word back that I would make time available to attend the reception. Bazarov's offices were on the top floor of the cold stone, and highly deceiving, two-story building near the ship. From outside, the edifice looked typically Odessan, rather old and drab. The first floor housed Soviet port officials who handled mail, arranged launches, supervised harbor control and a small radio station, gave instructions to pilots, and so on. These quarters were dank and stark, the floors made of those unevenly cut flagstones on which my wounded puppies had lain moaning. The grouting was poorly done—in short, typical Soviet construction. From the first floor a wide staircase led up to the second floor, but that floor always seemed off limits. There was an iron grate in front of the staircase, preventing people from entering. The gate was made of steel slats riveted together and compressed like an accordion. Until I attended the evening party, the protective device was always closed, with a small guarded door next to the grate. A Soviet soldier posted there might at best allow a single person of obviously high position to enter and mount the grand staircase, which one could view through the mesh of the gate. Made of better material than you normally saw in Russia—polished marble—the staircase was a good fifteen feet wide, providing ascension to what turned out to be a truly regal second floor.

Whenever I was involved in daytime port activities on the ground floor, I saw only a few high officials go upstairs, and not the usual first floor personnel. The whole thing seemed very secretive, reminding me of special western stores in Odessa, where guards similarly let only the most privileged Soviets enter.

Arriving at this building on the night of Bazarov's party, and well past normal office hours, I imbibed an eerie, ghost town atmosphere on the first floor. You walked down a dimly lit hallway toward the grand staircase, where a greater volume of light shone. Tonight the gate was rolled back, and a gentleman there, obviously security, was festively dressed and displayed no weapons, though perhaps packing something under his suit coat. Other people began arriving at the same time, foreigners of different nationalities, and Russian dignitaries from the city. Everyone was well dressed, myself included. I rarely carried a suit on vessels, but did have a uniform white shirt, with four-bar gold shoulder boards displaying my rank. I almost never wore that uniform shirt, except for rare occasions like this one. I also had on a pair of black slacks to match it.

Climbing the staircase, I reached a second story that made me feel like I'd left Russia and entered a world of luxury. It brought back the extravagant, gaudy atmosphere of Italian restaurants at home that people used for weddings and such. The entrance to the large hall, site of the party, and to the offices up here consisted of two hinged doors that met, swinging inward from the hall. On the outside these doors were constructed of heavy oak. The doorway was also trimmed with oak and with brass door knockers, highly polished and ornate. And of course there was a doorman.

On my arrival he ushered me in, and I was astounded at the thickness of that door's wood, plus about five inches of top quality leather secured with brass pins in the back of it. There must have been a good six inches of padding under that leather, obviously maintaining a soundproof atmosphere in here. How did I know this? Because until the guard opened the door, you couldn't hear anything inside, and then when it was open, the noise of the band and the crowd assaulted your ears!

Inside, too, the walls were done in oak, and bore more leather cushioning, and in the center of the hall was a fine crystal chandelier. Floors were made of highly polished marble, and expensive Persian rugs lay in different parts of the room. The furniture of antique quality must have been worth a small fortune. The entire hall of probably 50 feet by 100 (in length) had somewhat of an old Victorian look; but this was obviously KGB territory, making it feel more sinister to me. Even the windows had shutters on the inside that were probably as thick as the doors. When they were closed, it was easy to figure out that nobody on the outside would know what was transpiring in here. Opened, these windows would have given a fine view of the harbor.

Toward the end of the large rectangular hall were two doors, again ornate and trimmed in oak, one of which led into Bazarov's personal office. Shortly after I'd entered, Dimitri personally greeted me, with two of his minions and their wives at his side. I wasn't sure whether the KGB boss was married, for he seemed to have no liege companion on his arm. I suspected he wasn't, but instead, was something of a playboy. That night he didn't hesitate to scan the crop of invited females, and during conversations, he'd continue looking over the room, obviously not engrossed in his interlocutor's words as much as he was by the ladies.

During the first half hour or so, Dimitri escorted me about, introducing me to masters or senior officers from different vessels, as well as their wives, plus loyal Communist officials like the police chief, whom I'd met after the hotel fight. This time they acted cordial and relaxed. Tsar Bazarov set the tone of the party, and if he decided he'd be looser than normal, then many of the locals simply acted in kind. They always took their lead from the head man, careful not to do anything that would be criticized the next day. Vodka flowed freely, and caviar was generously dished out to the guests. Bazarov's favorite libation seemed to be lemon vodka, and on several occasions he asked me to partake as well. I refrained, as I didn't want to find myself weakened by such a formidable man. I knew Dimitri might be able to slurp his vodka and maintain his guile, but I wasn't sure of my own ability to do so. Instead, I drank tea—the Russians did make that beverage well, both green and black. To me it was a workable alternative to the coffee I indulged in too frequently then—typically drinking six or eight cups a day on ships.

Of course I was being careful that night in the KGB lair, and whenever I drank tea, it came from a community pot. I took no cup that was handed to me, nor did I allow attending servants to offer me drinks they brought around on a tray. Instead, I obtained my tea from a preparation area where everyone else was reaching for cups, remaining alert the entire night.

Bazarov and I did our initial buzzing around, chatting with people for about forty-five minutes, and at the end of the hour, I was introduced to a dapper American couple. The man was well-dressed and handsome, and his wife strikingly beautiful. Bob and Judy[13], as I'll call them, were the previously mentioned ship chandlers from Baton Rouge. Praising them lavishly, Bazarov explained how he had become fast friends with these Americans. He said that any time he was in the Mississippi Delta or lower Valley area, he would insist on his ship being supplied through these particular chandlers. He said he'd always enjoyed working with them, because they had high standards, including a taste for fine western cuisine. They also provided Bazarov their Mercedes whenever he was over there. In return, the relationship seemed to have lined Judy and Bob's pockets with Russian money.

We talked at length with the couple—about life in the States, how different it was from the Soviet Union, etc. Bazarov was very open, contrasting the amenities of western life with those of his motherland. We went on to light political talk and other hors d'oeuvreish topics; but I wanted to cut to the chase, finding out what would bring two classy Americans to Communist Odessa.

In a kind of group explanation—each finishing the others' sentences—the three indicated that Bazarov had invited them over through the Inflot Agency, providing a vacation in the Black Sea resort area at Soviet government expense. That barely whetted my appetite, and I pressed Bob more directly, asking him again what on earth could entice him and Judy to such a place? Even the north coast of Alaska provided better resort facilities! The weather, as noted, was problematic in Odessa—often in the low 60's and with the temperature of badly polluted water a good ten degrees below that. It simply made no sense to come here on a vacation, and I wanted to find out what was *really* going on.

Bob said that he and his wife had wanted to see Captain Bazarov's administrative headquarters, and what his position was in the Soviet system. So they were happy to accept his invitation, but sure, there were some comforts lacking in Communist Russia. All in all, however, they were enjoying themselves, and had one more week left in their visit.

---

[13]   These are pseudonyms.

I now began thinking of the timing of Bazarov's party, and felt sure that he had scheduled it expressly in the middle of Judy's and Bob's vacation. I wondered what he wanted to fish out of me, or perhaps tell me via these two Americans.

As the night wore on, Dimitri migrated to other corners of the hall, becoming increasingly drunk. The dinner they served was remarkably palatable, the only decent Russian food I'd eaten in the country. Bazarov must have known that he could not afford to offer a menu similar to what Party hacks had at places like the Krasny. The music played by a Russian ensemble of string instruments, sax, drummer, piano, French horn, and maybe a couple of trumpets was nice as well.

It became apparent that Bazarov's lemon vodka had now affected him—his face itself growing a bit yellow, and a red hue blooming on his nose. While he moved around, my new American friends, particularly Judy, sought me out on several occasions, even while I was engaged in other conversations. A blond southern belle, she wore a beautiful, low-cut evening gown—easily the best dressed of all the women here—and her husband could certainly be proud of her. Without a doubt she knew her powers, and in fact that's how she got my attention, giving me a gander while I was talking to someone else. It was like a signal that she wanted me to come over and hear something she had to say—something I needed to know.

So I tried casually to edge back into a comfortable conversational range with them, perhaps unnoticed by the inebriated Bazarov—but who knew? With her husband standing rather quietly at her side, Judy started talking from the hip, asking me whether I liked my job and whether there was any other type of work, besides shipboard duties, that I was doing while in Russia. She asked this rather covertly and slyly, and I returned the ball over the net, using her words: "Are *you* doing any other work here?" Her husband seemed worried, and he interrupted me near the end of my sentence, saying that "this is not the place to have such a discussion," adding: "Why don't you invite us to your ship for lunch tomorrow?"

To which I replied: "Sure, you can go ahead and make arrangements to come, but do me one favor: leave your pet Russian friend back in his cage, OK?" They both sprouted knowing half-smiles. After drinks and finger food hors d'oeuvres, then the meal and dancing, we had made it past midnight, and most of the officials and dignitaries were gone, thoroughly incapacitated by the booze that had flowed so freely. A Soviet chapter of MADD would have had a field day in the parking lot, slapping their bumper stickers on all these drivers' cars.

Since I was obviously the night's celebrity, I felt I should stick around till the end. With Bazarov, I thanked departing guests for coming. But the KGB chief was quite impaired, and the last few visitors left without him being at the door to see them off. By this time he had retired to his office sanctuary. Judy and Bob joined him there, and most of the staff had gone home. Dimitri's closest administrative assistant, his secretary, was still on hand, and as I said goodbye to the last of the guests, she motioned me toward his office. In front of that office was a rather large vestibule with a private bar and kitchenette area. Bazarov's assistant not only kept a watchful eye on anyone about to enter the office, but also acted as a butler. Once in his lair, Dimitri could request drinks and small snack foods for any invited honchos. He now ushered me into this inner sanctum, probably as splendid as any corporate CEO's in the States. The floor was fully covered with very thick carpet, and you almost needed snowshoes to get across it.

Despite his condition Bazarov struck up a pointed conversation with me, his curiosity fairly jumping out of him. Very direct, he wanted to know how I could have attained my position in such short order, indicating that while I had been talking to the final guests, he and his American friends had been discussing that very matter. He said they were all equally intrigued by my rapid ascent. I, in turn, was interested that Bazarov would speak on behalf of Bob and Judy, and now began to wonder what tomorrow's luncheon appointment would expose to me.

In answer to the query about rank, I explained that I had been in the right place at the right time, that I'd always worked hard at my jobs, and that owners trusted me with their substantial investments. I was speaking truthfully here. Remember, again, that once you entered Soviet waters, no communication was possible with the West, so I was last and final judge as to what would be done re ships' operations— including crew member behavior, cargo handling, movements of the vessel, etc. Bazarov knew that added up to a large responsibility, but he remained dissatisfied with my response. He said he had never met someone so young with this kind of weighty appointment. I asked whether there was something in that which made him suspicious. Rather backhandedly, he replied: "No Lance, I wouldn't question anything with regard to your job duties or assignments." I then thanked Dimitri for providing me a car and driver—I said I had not overlooked these special attentions he had given me in Odessa. Thankfully there wasn't only Boris, the chauffeur, to show me the ropes, but other friends who looked in on me from time to time (of course I meant the bugging at the Marisk!). With a laugh I told Comrade Bazarov that he ought perhaps to improve the hotel's phone system, due to the static and noise of people talking in the background. Bob and Judy couldn't contain themselves, and began laughing themselves.

At which point I turned my head, asking Bob whether they had the same problem where they were staying. "And by the way," I added, "where *are* you staying? The Marisk?" They shook their heads, informing me that they were at a private *dacha*, which Dimitri had kindly provided them. Bazarov had now begun losing interest. However much he may have wanted to draw me out that night, he didn't get very far. He was so wasted by this time that his chin lay in his hand and his elbow on the desk. Trying to keep going, his conversation ricocheted off the palm of his hand.

The party ended when Dimitri's executive assistant came in, declaring that he had had too much liquor, and that it was time to leave. I now wondered whether Bazarov was in control of this operation, or whether she was. I never found out her name, was never introduced to her, and it struck me that she might well be the power behind the throne here. Powerful women *could* make it to high places in the Soviet Union—Vida's mother being a case in point.

The following day my American lunch guests duly arrived at the ship, chauffeured by another KGB agent in civilian garb. But there was a delay at the bottom of the gangway, where apparently the Russian guard would not let them pass. One of my officers informed me of a verbal scrap involving two well-dressed people and maybe two Russians busy screaming at each other. I realized these must be my guests and went down to greet them. Approaching, I heard the KGB chauffeur, very red-faced, bring his voice upward in an irate crescendo, apparently giving an ultimatum in Russian to the gangway guard: "Let these two Yanks come through, or I'll have your hide" was the apparent message. The guard finally acquiesced, snapping to and saluting the official.

Bob and Judy then came up the gangway, and I greeted them on the main deck, asking what had transpired down there. To which they replied: "Just a small misunderstanding. The guard thought we were Russians, and since we didn't have appropriate passes, our chauffeur had to explain what was going on. They wanted to be sure that we weren't trying for asylum." I noticed that during the argument Bob and Judy hadn't spoken any Russian, in which they were fluent (I'd heard them using the language at the party). They obviously didn't want the gangway guard to be aware of their conversational verve in that language. They had simply left the argument entirely up to the chauffeur, which told me they knew he was more than just a driver or flunky. They must have known that when the soldier heeded the ultimatum and saluted, he didn't want to mess with that fellow's power.

Having won the day, the chauffeur headed up the gangway, too, as though invited to lunch. But I had Bob and Judy convey my regrets— to the effect that this was a private party. Proceeding back down the gangway, the official waited by his vehicle.

When we arrived in the ship's stateroom, I arranged to have lunch served immediately by the ship's steward, and Bob and Judy seemed happy to have it. They were dressed casually but well, she in black leather pants, he in brand new blue jeans and open shirt. The atmosphere was comfortable for all of us. Over lunch Bob and Judy encouraged me not to be so rough on Bazarov, that I must understand that he was in a difficult and precarious position, and should he screw up, it would create problems for them as well. His position was one of wanting to be friendly with me, but also having to protect his own power base by not letting any information slip into western hands under his watch. I was intrigued, asking Bob and Judy directly if they were here to convey something to me, which I should then take back to the West. I still found the timing of this whole business unusual.

Was Dimitri Bazarov, in fact, a double agent? Was that why he was always being difficult and sparring with me, trying to maintain his good KGB credentials? Was he actually trying to deliver some sort of message to me? I thought again of the party's timing and the invitation of Bob and Judy to Russia.

It turned out that the soldier at the bottom of the gangway shouldn't have let them on board, because they did indeed have something to offer me. In the presence of her husband, Judy handed me a sealed envelope, asking me to put it personally in the ship's safe. Which was more complicated than you might think. Whenever a ship entered the Soviet Union, a special shoreside officer immediately came on board and entered the office containing the safe. He then affixed a paper seal to it, so that you could not open that safe while in Russia. Just before sailing away from port, officials would come on board, checking to see that the seal was still intact. If broken, there was hell to pay, and a delay involving weeks of investigation.

It was now evident by what Bob and Judy had told me that they were here for more than just a vacation. I realized they had something to deliver that was important. In my original contact made prior to leaving the States, I'd been told that at some point there might be some information passed to me—something beyond my coffee cup business, of which I needed to be aware. Bazarov couldn't afford to compromise his position by passing such information directly to me, or even using any of his citizens to do so. So he was obviously using American proxies.

The easiest way to get it out of the country would be by using the ship's safe. But how could I break the seal? With a smile on his face Bob pulled out another envelope and this one he opened. It contained a perfect duplicate seal—with the same officer's signature on it. So within a matter of a few minutes we removed the old seal, I put the envelope in the safe, and I carefully glued the new seal over the gum spots made by the previous one. No one would have been able to tell the difference. And with that I walked my friends down to the head of the gangway, watching them drive off with their KGB chauffeur. In the distance, my friend Boris sat in his own car, resting.

Returning to the ship's office, I wondered what our safe might now contain. But mastering my curiosity, I opened up my briefcase, loading it with a bag of Orville Redenbacher's fine popcorn, then went off to see Lev and Vida. The situation at the bottom of the gangway amused me, for the guard who had been so fussy about letting Bob and Judy on board was the type who would also be invariably suspicious about my briefcase contents. Now he seemed doubly curious! This is the mentality of a spy society. He probably thought I had important documents on me, and if he is reading this today, he now knows that all I had inside was American popcorn! He would dearly have loved to open that briefcase, but owing to my diplomatic immunity, he couldn't do it. So I took the case to Lev's and Vida's, and only there did I work the combination, removing my booty.

I knew that my relationship with Bazarov would remain antagonistic, but also felt that a huge bridge had been crossed between him and me. I now figured Dimitri to be a double agent, working both sides of the street. The CIA obviously knew they were going to get some information from him. It made perfect sense that the Soviets were more vulnerable to the threat of double agents, due to their material needs and general insatiability. They had the same desire of all humans to have more and better things. But I knew I could not change my way of handling Mr. B. I simply couldn't afford to compromise either his position or mine. Who knew what he was *really* doing? To keep his KGB credentials intact, he probably had to take a fish or two from time to time, showing his bosses that he was catching those who had to be nabbed. To this day I don't know whether Dimitri had done something inappropriate when Bob and Judy passed their envelope to me.

I do know that when I got back to the States, the two CIA agents I had originally met paid me another call, and when they asked if I had something for them, I handed them the envelope. With a kind of handheld magnifying glass, they carefully examined their prize, running all the seams of the envelope under it, before leaving my office, satisfied that I hadn't tampered with it. I had realized that I should leave well enough alone, and not play games with my future. But that future certainly contained more bumps in the road!

Chapter 10

Ships' Revolvers and Revolts

A T sea on the *Golden Endeavor*, about midway through 1980, I was tested again not by the KGB, but by an irate crew member who decided to carve up another crew member, much like a Christmas turkey. This battle took place down in the ship's galley living quarters of the stern area, and the instigator was quite successful, leaving his prey severely wounded and bleeding, before he ran to the forecastle. On arrival there, he went through the watertight doors, locking himself in, and for reasons involving the ship's safety, I knew I had to flush him out. In the area where he was barricaded there were a lot of volatile chemicals and paints that he could easily ignite. And that seemed a real possibility, since the man had evidently lost his mind!

So I had to resort to the use of some heat—i.e., the ship's revolver(s). When it came to the latter, crew members were always aware that the captain had one on board. But they didn't know that in many cases the ship carried *two* revolvers. With that in mind it occurred to me one day that it might be prudent to keep one loaded, and one empty. I made sure I could readily identify the loaded gun, marking at least one with a white, three-ring reinforcing thing, right by the trigger housing. Given that these revolvers were dark blue or cobalt color, the identification stood out easily. My logic was that in the event of an insurrection on a ship, I would be required to hand the extra revolver over to one of my officers to help subdue miscreants on board. But since you couldn't always know which officers were loyal, I could proffer my unloaded gun as a kind of insurance measure.

This stratagem unexpectedly helped me with my barricaded, irate crew member. Above the compartment where he was holed up was a hatchway, from which we could gain access. There were also two doors coming in from the main deck, which he'd used for his initial entry. Both were dog-downed, i.e., locked from inside, making entry from the outside difficult and time-consuming. I instructed the chief officer and the other ship's officers to come with me to flush out this crazy. Taking both revolvers, the loaded and unloaded ones, I conceived a plan to decoy him, instructing the officers to make noise at the door entries which the perpetrator had gone through, in order to divert his attention; meanwhile, the chief officer would open the hatch above him. As soon as the hatch was open, I knew he would see the shaft of light it brought to the compartment where he was hiding, and that he might attack or kill whoever came in after him. There was a straight ladder that I would have to use to get down to that compartment, but I had no intention of going in there.

Instead, I took the empty revolver and dropping it down the open hatch, suddenly cursed loudly, shouting to the chief officer, "Oh my God, I dropped my damned revolver!" In a flash the mad dog grabbed the gun, and with a broad smile on his face pointed it up at me, shouting: "Now I got your ass, Captain!" The chief officer was unaware of my plan and when I glanced at his face, it looked as though he was having apoplexy! Calmly, I talked to the idiot standing at the bottom of the ladder, telling him to come out of there before he hurt somebody, or got himself hurt. And he cackled back: "Oh yeah? I got your *gun*, Captain. Now what are you going to do? I'm coming out of here and you guys are going to run!"

Suddenly I reached behind my back, put my hand under my shirt-tails, and pulled out the loaded revolver. Pointing it at him, I suggested he look carefully at the other gun's barrel and magazine, asking if he could count the bullets in the cylinder. He laughed and said, "Why?", still pointing the empty gun at me. And I responded: "Because when I look at your gun, I don't see anything in the cylinders." He hesitated for a second, long enough for me to tell him that he had a count of three to decide which one was loaded and which one wasn't.

Pondering, he finally decided it was best to drop his gun on the deck, climb up the ladder, and surrender. When he did, we immediately put him in irons, constraining him for several days and placing him on a diet of bread and water, then a legal punishment. On arrival at our destination we handed him over to the American consul. I had never thought things would happen that way, more concerned about possible shipboard revolts, and whether my officers would be with or against me.

Another interesting gun episode occurred after the previous incident. I was still employed by Apex Marine, headquartered in Lake Success, N.Y., and on the *Golden Endeavor*. My "port captain" was a Greek who did not hold an American license and had never sailed on a U.S. vessel before, and it quickly became apparent that he knew little or nothing of what needed to be done on an American ship. He lacked working knowledge of supertankers and had a sparse background in maritime matters generally. However, this scrawny, sawed-off fellow of maybe 5'6", with heavy Greek accent and olive complexion, had a personality allowing him to play the role of an Aristotle Onassis type, as though he owned the ships, when basically, he was a mailboy messenger! It was not unusual for this Spyridon[14] to come on board ship, disturbing us when we were under time constraints to get cargo loaded or unloaded, or other operational complications intervened. Spyridon would simply hang around, lacking any technical knowledge or working experience of that sort of vessel, and so his recommendations were generally off the wall and troublesome even to entertain, given the loss of time they engendered. He always had an air of arrogance, at which I openly laughed. Whenever he came on board, I enjoyed pulling his tail feathers, for he acted exactly like a rooster in a barnyard. He'd crow and make a lot of noise and tell everyone how important he was, and then I'd play a trick on him or simply give him a hard time. He would threaten—often once a day—to fire me, then I'd say, "You'd better take the ship out to sea," and he'd disappear down the gangway, as by law he couldn't do that, and in any event, had no command capability.

There was one particular incident I remember involving this fellow—another of my gun stories. We were in port in Galveston, Texas with this "Captain" Spyridon. (We had given him the title of "Captain," though the only ship he'd ever skippered was probably his bathtub!) While in Galveston he was in my office at about 9:30 or 10 in the morning. We'd just returned from breakfast at officers' mess, and he and I were sitting in my office with the door open, having a conversation.

Without any warning a ship's crew member—the pumpman whose responsibility was to handle some of the cargo pumps, i.e., a non-officer—dashed into my office with a knife in hand, and a manic, fiery look on his face. He shouted loudly at maybe ten feet from me and ten feet equidistant from Spyridon that he wanted to know the location of another crew member, whom he obviously wished to harm seriously. His outburst caught me off guard, but I remained casual, leaning back in my soft leather captain's chair. Before answering the question, I glanced over at Spyridon cowering in a corner of the room, fear scribbled all over his face. He had made unusual haste to get from one end of the settee to the other, giving him an extra five feet of distance from the irate pumpman. But he also knew he was cornered and hugged the wall in terror. This was the same puffed-up guy who would always try to impress you with his nautical credentials, experience, and tales of

---

14   This is a pseudonym.

courage. I should add that Spyridon was nearly twenty years my senior. I was then in my early thirties, he was in his mid to late forties.

Anyway, I heard the crazed pumpman holler at me again: "Where is that damned deckhand who's supposed to be on watch?" Then I jumped from my chair and standing straight up, with a slight forward lean of my shoulders, shouted back at him: "You're not getting any answers unless you give me the courtesy of proper entry procedure! Now get out of this office!" I further told him to shut the door, and to knock on it if he wished to re-enter. Probably in his early fifties, the pumpman obviously had a real problem with the deckhand he'd mentioned, and I knew as well that he had a problem with the bottle. Since we'd been in port twenty-four hours, he had probably stocked up on booze and was now displaying his valor, due to a blood alcohol count obviously spinning out of control.

For some reason he decided to apologize, closed the door, and then knocked. This interval gave me time to reach into the top drawer of my desk, pulling out a .38. Given my system, I had to reaffirm that this was indeed the loaded gun, not the unloaded one. Meanwhile, I glanced over my shoulder, watching Spyridon going nuts! He was stammering something unintelligible, and I even thought I detected an odor of urine emanating from his direction. The pumpman kept knocking, I returned to my chair, and putting the revolver in the top drawer of the desk but keeping my hand on it, called out: "Come in!" The pumpman reappeared, his angry routine unchanged, shouting that he *wanted* that deckhand. His knife was still open, probably a five-inch blade. He continued making demands and I told him curtly: "You aren't getting any answers till you put down your knife." Ignoring my request, he kept waving the weapon, screaming that he was going to cut the deckhand to pieces because he was tired of the guy messing with his head! Apparently there was an ongoing dispute here that I hadn't previously noticed. In a quieter tone, but with more intensity and firmness, I told him again: "Put down the knife!"

At that point I drew my hand out of the drawer, pointing the .38 at him. Because of my position in the room I couldn't see Spyridon, since I had to watch the pumpman's moves. I still remained seated in a somewhat casual position, leaning slightly back in the leather chair, with my revolver pointed at this irate fellow. From the cowering Spyridon's direction, the smell seemed even stronger now!

It seemed quite a while that the pumpman stayed put, trying to analyze the situation, and finally he laughed and said: "Captain, I wasn't going to do nothin' to hurt you," and put the knife down on the floor. I responded that I knew he had no intention of hurting me and glancing over my shoulder at Spyridon, continued speaking to the pumpman: "Now to answer your question: I don't know where the deckhand is. But I have something else to tell you. I want you to go below and pack your gear and in thirty minutes get your ass back up to my office, because you're fired!" I then lifted the phone, calling the chief officer and instructing him to send one of the junior officers to assist the pumpman with his imminent departure.

About a half hour later the junior officer assigned this duty prodded the pumpman back into my office, whereupon I paid him off. Just as he was about to leave to exit the ship, turning his back and starting to walk out, I said: "By the way, I've got a present for you." Pulling the revolver out of my desk drawer, I opened up the magazine, extricating the bullet I would have used to kill him. "Take this as a souvenir," I told him. "You may want to put it on a chain, to remind yourself that this was what you were about to get this morning. Here...." With that the junior officer smiled broadly, and the pumpman was escorted off the ship, and out of my life.

Of course Spyridon found this a highly interesting way of dealing with such matters. But I sometimes wondered what *he* would have done had he really been a commander. To command you need among other things, a certain stability in your life, and this Greek fellow was a heavy-duty party hound. Each night when the ship was in port, he'd be out carousing and doing things I eschewed, having duties the next day.

But you guessed it: within a few hours—such is the short duration of human gratitude—Spyridon fired me yet again, which usually resulted in me being reinstated within another five minutes. It was a standing joke or wager on our ship—how many times you'd get fired by this buffoon while still in port. But it was just a joke, because the man himself was a joke. It was his vaudeville act, I guess....

One individual's violent behavior was of course easier to deal with than a conspiracy of several, which leads me to a more serious incident from this era. By 1983 I was working for a company called MTL—Marine Transport Lines—which had a contract with the U.S. Navy to operate specialized "sealift tankers," carrying a variety of fuels to military bases and operational fleets around the world. These ships hauled different categories of jet fuels—JP-4, JP-5, JP-8—used in various types of aircraft, as well as for propulsion on ships. I even carried a top-secret fuel for the SR-71, or the *Blackbird*. That fuel was manufactured exclusively by Exxon and formulated under top secret conditions, and with very stringent standards applied. It was used for only one aircraft application—on the U.S. Air Force SR-71, the fastest plane ever built.

Primarily used to overfly the Soviet Union and Communist China, this plane was outfitted with high resolution cameras and flew at such altitudes and speeds, that it could actually outfly any missile fired at it. Only two locations in the world based these planes—one at Okinawa and the other up the East Coast of England near the port of Grimsby. The fuel was loaded in Houston, Texas. A ship's captain needed to have top secret clearance even to handle this cargo, and during loading operations special U.S. Navy security was perimetered around the vessel. Tanks had to be meticulously hand-cleaned, with absolutely no moisture permitted in them. The fuel was so clear that when you looked into the tanks, you couldn't actually tell the liquid levels. So we used special gauges to determine when tanks were full, or approaching capacity. This was the purest form of kerosene ever developed, continually monitored for signs of moisture. A total lack of moisture was crucial, because when the plane flew at such high altitudes any moisture in the fuel would freeze, and even the slightest water crystal could cause fuel lines to plug. This would ultimately result in engine failure, and a crash.

The uniqueness of the plane's design was such that at speeds it flew, its wings needed to have a kind of capillary cooling system. As in a car's radiator, the fuel itself was used to keep the wings from becoming too hot and burning up. So it was pulled from the fuel tanks, out across the wings, and then into the engines. This served two purposes: to moderate the metal temperatures of the wings and to preheat the gas, so that when it entered the engine it was in a highly combustible state.

Given that these were the kinds of cargoes we carried, and because I had the additional responsibility of special clearance, I was ultra-careful choosing engineering and deck officer staff. At one point my original chief engineer had to leave the ship in an emergency, and a new chief engineer I hadn't met was assigned to replace him. His name was Robert Fowler.[15] The company sent no profile on this Fowler, so I found myself in the dark as to his engineering abilities, that is, concerning main propulsion systems and marine diesel applications generally.

When Fowler arrived on board, I had a lengthy discussion with him about his background, feeling a bit uneasy because he seemed to lack sufficient experience on diesel-powered vessels. He assured me that

---

[15] This is a pseudonym.

by law he had all requisite qualifications to perform his duties on this kind of ship, and was more than capable. Before leaving port, I nonetheless called the company, expressing concerns about the man and indicating that I would be closely monitoring the entire engineering staff. At least our first assistant engineer was well qualified, with several years under his belt on a diesel-powered vessel. But the second assistant engineer had also newly joined our ship, and he, too, lacked experience.

Once having left port and proceeded out to sea, it wasn't long before I realized that the chief engineer knew *nothing* concerning diesels and had no control over his department. As a result he was totally at the mercy of the other engineers on board. An older man, probably in his early sixties, Fowler seemed very shaky. He had worked with the MSTS operations, an outcropping of the U.S. Navy, but primarily in a civilian capacity. However, even from an administrative point of view he appeared totally inept. Overtime basically went unregulated, his explanations about why repairs were needed and what kinds were being undertaken seemed illogical, and despite my limited engineering background, I could see that Fowler was way over his head in his position. Further inquiry informed me that he was indeed newly hired, and that this was his first assignment with the company. The shoreside engineering staff admitted that they might have overlooked a few things in inquiring about the fellow's resumé!

So I was stuck, henceforth deciding to meet with Fowler regularly, in order to review procedures in the engine room—atypical for a captain to do. I was fortunate that my chief officer was an energetic young man, well suited for his position, and that he was able to execute duties without much supervision. But as time went on, friction developed between that chief officer, whose main responsibility was shipboard cargo operations, and the engineering support staff, including the second assistant engineer, the other man bereft of qualifications for his position. Relations between this second assistant engineer and the chief officer heated up, and the latter informed me that he was getting little cooperation from the second assistant, and that his requests to have the chief engineer intervene had also fallen on deaf ears.

Observing for myself this increasing friction, I realized that we were in a dire situation, particularly owing to the kind of cargo we carried. I noticed a lethal factionalism developing on the vessel. The second assistant and chief engineers would spend long hours together at night and well into the morning, either in Fowler's office, or in the second assistant's cabin. In more and more instances I had to call on the first assistant engineer to handle questions regarding the ship's engines and such. This first assistant and I began to communicate more and more, for it was obvious that the chief engineer could barely screw in a light bulb! The second assistant engineer was virtually useless as well.

In his late twenties, of stocky build and about 5'10", this second assistant engineer was one of life's intimidators, trying to camouflage his ignorance via loud talking and displays of arrogance, which in most cases succeeded in scaring people off. His immediate staff was certainly cowed. The man's M.O. with Fowler was similar, so that the chief engineer became something of a puppet of this young blowhard. Needless to say, such personalities are detrimental to a ship's overall performance, creating human undercurrents that can hamper efficient operations.

The second assistant and chief engineer distanced themselves from the first assistant engineer, because the latter could see through them and they knew it. This first assistant was a man in his late fifties, a white-haired fellow with heavy Norwegian brogue, though American. At about 6'1", there was no question he could handle himself in a physical confrontation. I had to commit totally to him, since the other two men were such imbeciles! I also trusted him, because I felt he was honest with me, but only insofar as he responded to my questions without varnishing the truth. However, this first assistant never volunteered information on various engineering problems that might be occurring, and which only came up after I really pushed. He never sketched out what was truly happening down in the engine room, which frustrated me, for I had an important mission to carry out, one requiring a high standard of performance.

Things finally got so bad during my regular interplay with Chief Engineer Fowler that he began to lie in response to administrative questions I posed—not to mention engineering queries, which I knew he couldn't answer. Fowler's answers became so off the wall that I threatened to log him at the end of our voyage for dereliction of duty, instituting an inquiry with the U.S. Coast Guard. I hoped this warning would straighten him out, but apparently, it only inspired more late-night meetings with the headstrong second assistant.

About a week after my warnings I caught Fowler in a flagrant lie, finally deciding to log him officially, which required that he present himself in my office. As a witness to these proceedings I summoned the chief officer. I then logged the chief engineer for flagrantly lying to the master, for dereliction of duty, and for a number of other lesser actions.

About two hours after Fowler had been dismissed, the second assistant engineer burst into my office, screaming that I had no business logging his friend, and that he was going to make damn sure that the union patrolman found out about this high-handed behavior! I could barely contain my amusement and in fact, I didn't. Sitting behind my desk and with a broad smile on my face, I told the young egotist that if he didn't get out of my office on the count of three, I'd log *him*, too— for as many misdeeds as I could tote up. I figured the second assistant could count, but apparently he didn't want to, so when I reached "three," I picked up the phone, called the chief officer into my cabin, which was required by law, then logged the second assistant engineer for insubordination, unruliness, and incompetence, citing several occasions where he had failed to fulfill his duties on the ship.

He became predictably furious, demanding his right to a statement, which I granted him, as I had Fowler. We also recorded his rantings and ravings in the ship's official log. I then told him to leave my office, which he did, but only after whispering something under his breath which I might have construed as a threat—that is, had I wanted to press the issue and put him in irons. However, I elected to ignore it, knowing I was dealing with a real bag of hot air.

To complete an unruly triumvirate on the ship, we now need to discuss my radio officer, another strange bird. This guy was a Vietnam War relic, and because I myself had spent time there, his "authentic" war stories dispensed in the officers' ward room at mealtimes never impressed me. On several occasions facts he cited seemed inconsistent with locations and dates of events with which I was familiar. It appeared he superimposed himself as some type of hero in those events, times and places where he could not possibly have been. I was aware, too, that he liked his liquor, and usually when we were in port, and he was released from ship duties, he managed to get himself thoroughly soused, arriving back in the nick of time to sober up before sailing again.

After the two logging episodes mentioned, table arrangements in the officers' mess appeared to change slightly. The radio officer now began sitting with the disgraced second assistant and chief engineers. Actually I could have cared less with whom these men ate; in fact, if I could have, I would have set up a special ward room for them alone.

But one day the radio officer questioned me as to why the chief engineer and his second assistant had been logged, which I considered an intrusion into my command jurisdiction. A lengthy discussion with the radio officer ensued in my quarters, on his meddling in ship's operations which didn't concern him. I explained that I wasn't excited by his performance either, and that if he wanted to join his two new pals and be logged, I could easily accommodate him. I further exposed him for his lying concerning those obviously concocted stories about his Vietnam War record. I now warned him that he had better stick to his duties alone, and to stop commiserating with an inept chief engineer and second assistant. Then I dismissed him from my office.

That private conversation took place in mid-afternoon, and I hoped the man would heed my advice. But at the evening meal the trio sat together again, mumbling and grumbling, and intermittently throwing baleful glances my way. I got the impression that they were quite unhappy, knowing I was still living and functioning aboard this vessel.

Eventually I would learn that they had decided that evening to discuss their rights under law, in a private meeting to take place in the radio officer's cabin. This meeting apparently included light beverages which, however, had alcoholic content. Apparently it started shortly after dinner, continuing on into the wee hours of morning. And apparently, it reached a point where they decided they were going to notify shoreside American authorities of my overbearing ship management. The triumvirate seemed to have concluded that I and old Captain Bly had a lot in common. No longer would they stand for this upstart captain telling them what to do and how to do it.

About four a.m. I heard from the bridge watch officer that there was a call from the company on our satellite phone. Telephone communication in that era had just begun, and was used only in real emergencies, so the call was unexpected. I thought perhaps that there was some worldwide upheaval, and that I might receive special instructions concerning a secret rendezvous with a naval escort.

To my surprise the company's chief operating officer for MTL asked: "Captain, is everything all right on board?" I was taken off guard, and responded, "Yes, everything's fine. Why would you ask such a question?" He replied that the U.S. Coast Guard and naval military authorities had received a message emanating from our ship about an hour earlier, indicating that there were problems on board. He told me that as of that time the company had not yet received a transcript of the message, but the authorities had asked him whether I still had command control of the ship.

Hearing these words I immediately felt goose bumps run down my back and all the way to my legs, for it was obvious that something serious was afoot. But I wasn't 100% sure where the danger was coming from. The company official reiterated the necessity of proving that I had command of the ship. He said the message they received had apparently led authorities to believe there was some kind of insurrection on the ship. I listened to him—and was absolutely floored. He further stated that the U.S. Navy had dispatched a heavy cruiser that would be in my last known position within the next six hours to assist me in whatever way necessary. They would have boarding parties ready, so I must immediately unearth the nature of the problems on my vessel.

Once again, he asked: "Do you have control of the ship?" Then he added: "Lance, if they've got a gun to your head, don't let on to the fact that I've been asking you this question." Listening to him in the dark, and knowing my second officer was next to me, overhearing my conversation along with two deck hands, I felt reasonably sure that if there had been some insurrection, I would have been aware by now that I'd lost command of the ship. So I responded to the company official that I felt everything was OK and that he should call my wife, explaining the situation to her and asking for the secret code word we used for our home security system. It worked on the principle that if someone broke into our house and the system was breached, then a monitoring agency would call the house, and if the person answering the phone didn't give the agency the code word, police would be immediately dispatched. I figured there was one way I could reassure all outside parties that I had command of the ship: by having this company officer, whom my wife knew, ask her for that code word. Once he knew the code word, and if I gave the same one, that would mean I still had control of the ship. (The code word was "king's kids.") I told the company official I now needed to hang up, that precious time was passing, and if something was indeed developing below decks, I needed to get to the ship's armory as soon as possible.

The reason there was an armory on board was because this was the U.S. Navy ship *China Sea*. The Navy had arranged to turn over some support vessels to the Merchant Marine in order to reduce its operating costs. Officers and crew would not be under the Navy's command, other than for the charter party business agreement, and I was not obliged to countermand either the Merchant Marine, or international or U.S. maritime law. But because this *was* a Navy ship, we fortunately had a small arms locker on board, to which I had full access. At times like this the Navy expected me to go ahead and use it.

So I now called up the ship's chief officer, whose loyalty I didn't doubt, instructing him to meet me by the arms cache. Once I arrived at the armory door, I told him to stand lookout, making sure that no one rushed us, while I quickly opened up to grab two revolvers and two shotguns. The third officer was another young man I considered trustworthy, and I brought him along to help us search the ship for problems. The first location I needed to visit was the radio room, and by this time my thoughts were sufficiently collected that I was suspicious of the chief engineer, the second assistant engineer—and the radio officer.

It is, by the way, illegal to transmit messages from a ship at sea without the captain's express approval. So it was apparent that whatever the stage of a possible insurrection, the rebels had control of the radio room and transmitter location, and had enrolled the radio officer as a co-conspirator, or else had threatened his life in order for him to have communicated with authorities. As was true for every door on the ship, I had a passkey that would open up the radio room, and I now instructed the chief officer and third officer on how I wanted to attack that location. Loading both shotguns with a full clip of double-O buckshot, I knew how effective such weapons were in close-range fighting. In fact, *the* most efficient weapon in close quarters combat remains the 12-gauge shotgun, filled with buckshot.

Carefully, I approached the door to the radio room, instructing the two back-up officers to steer clear of the firing path I would need on opening the door. With one hand I turned the key and slammed the door open; with the other I brought a gun barrel down off my hip, pointing directly at the mid-body of what I took to be the radio officer, sleeping under several blankets in his bunk. He was so fully covered that I wasn't sure initially whether this was a ruse or not, and whether someone else I couldn't see might be standing in a corner of the room. Not proceeding any further, I shouted at the bulge in the blankets, "Get up! Stand on the floor!" I saw some movement and my finger was heavy on the trigger as the blankets began rustling. The radio officer's head swung around and he hollered in somewhat of a drunken stupor: "What the hell's goin' on?" I told him again to get up slowly and put his feet on the floor. The blanket slipped off him as he stood up, and I saw that he was unarmed. He stood in his boxer shorts with the blanket now dropped around his feet. I told him not to move and remained in the doorway with the shotgun aimed at him. I wasn't playing around. At this point I instructed the chief officer to open an adjacent door into the radio transmission room behind me, checking for signs of humans there. In a loud, firm voice I announced: "Don't hesitate to fire on anyone in there!" The radio officer began complaining that he was cold, and wanted to put his clothes on. I told him to keep quiet and to stand where he was, until I was sure the radio room was under my control.

Everything checked out OK, so I stepped into the radio officer's room, cautiously looking for other people. Once I was sure we were alone, I motioned the radio officer into the transmitting location, demanding to know what message had been sent from this vessel without my authority. He denied knowing anything about that, but after I insisted he take a long look at the barrel of my shotgun, his memory cleared up, and he began to weep. He told me that yes, he had sent a message, and I asked on whose authority he had done so. He said that it had been necessary to prevent me from abusing ship's officers and crew. At that point I called the third officer, still waiting in the passageway and holding the ship's handcuffs and leg irons, and instructed him to get the radio officer dressed, then shackle his ankles together, plus chain his left wrist to the chair, in front of the radio transmitter's station. When the radio officer was shackled, I told the third officer to lock himself in the room with him, and not to leave without my permission.

Having secured the radio room, I could now start searching the ship for the other insurrectionists. I proceeded down one deck to the engineering officers' level, locating the second assistant and chief engineer, both thoroughly drunk in Fowler's office. When the second assistant saw me arrive with shotgun in hand, he decided to confess about actions taken earlier that night, perceiving that there was now a big problem here, and that he was at its epicenter! The chief engineer told him to shut up, then I placed both under house arrest, each confined to his own cabin and neither permitted to speak to anyone on board, until I allowed it. I left the chief officer in charge of the engineering area, believing I had uncovered the core of the revolt. My concern at the time was simply to be sure that no other crew members were in league with these three conspirators. So I walked through crew's quarters, noticing nothing unusual, and smelling no alcohol.

Whereupon I returned to the bridge, called the company official on the satellite phone, communicated the code word which he had received from my wife, and reassured him thereby that the ship was still under my command. I further explained that upon our arrival in the Persian Gulf we would require replacements for the chief engineer, second assistant engineer, and radio officer.

It needs to be underlined that all this took place during a special mission bringing us into then hostile territory of the Persian Gulf, with the Iran-Iraq War raging, further elevating my concern during the entire episode. When we arrived off the coast of Oman, I had already notified the American consul that whether or not replacements were available for these officers, they were going to be sent off the ship and charged with insurrection. The consul took them into custody, and I later heard that they had to travel several days by camel to reach a major city, from which they would be flown back to the States. Months later I would meet the three conspirators in a legal proceeding where all were found guilty, losing officers' licenses and privileges. They would never again work on an American ship.

The whole episode had, however, made me queasy and anxious, because if there had been a full-blown insurrection on the ship, it would have required a difficult, bloody battle to regain control. But I *was* relieved when I finally realized that these birds' courage had come from the bottle, and that as I had presumed, they were cowards at heart. If potentially lethal ones....

Chapter 11

Final Diagnosis—
Lunacy On Board Ship!

BEFORE that revolt, an episode had occurred on the *Golden Endeavor* that fittingly concludes this account—a psychiatrist himself going crazy on board! The skipper I was relieving for this voyage had indicated prior to his departure that a Dr. Casper W. Kalbfuss[16] would be joining our ship. Kalbfuss was a friend of one of the company's owners and had induced this executive to allow him on an ocean voyage. So after I had reassumed command of the tanker, and the day before leaving port, a tall, thin, almost emaciated-looking fellow in his late forties arrived at my cabin. Kalbfuss had his practice on Long Island, near where the company owners lived, and had apparently taken a kind of sabbatical, handing his work off to associates. His goal, as I understood it, was to study the effect on humans of inhabiting large ships for extended periods of time.

As soon as we left port, I sat down with this Casper, giving him basic instructions on shipboard routines—safety matters regarding areas where he could move on the vessel, use of hardhats, and the like. He explained his idea of studying the mens' behavior patterns, and I said that if it didn't interfere with their work, it was fine by me. Even then he could be a silent observer, as long as he didn't disrupt operations by his presence. Dr. Kalbfuss agreed to this general plan.

Giving him the owner's cabin, which was as comfortable as my own stateroom, I said that I'd meet with him once a day, generally after supper, to hear his insights and how the project was going. Initially I hoped someone in his profession might enlighten me on the psychological problems I'd so often run into on ships! I myself had no doubt that the stresses of working on a floating island, where people are constrained for long periods of time, show up in behavior patterns which I'd certainly come to know well. However, I wasn't sure that this doctor—an educated, refined man probably unaware of the "dregs" effect—quite realized what he had gotten himself into here.

---

[16]   This is a pseudonym.

His conversation was laced with pedantic terminology, and I'd often have to stop him, asking the meaning of words he had used. No doubt he was highly educated school-wise, but was he educated in life? However, I tried not to caution him or to direct his thinking concerning the human specimens he would meet. I wanted him to find out things for himself, making his own observations and judgments.

Kalbfuss intended to stay with us for three months, a little short of the average voyage time (most crew members were on board between 100-180 days). He seemed to be a Type A personality, very meticulous, and from the start, overdressed for this milieu—with creases in his pants, wing-tipped shoes on his feet that were difficult to get around in, and so forth. Eventually I got him more appropriate clothing from the ship's "slop chest," where captains made a bit of extra money selling toiletries, snacks, and other items to crew and officers. The term "slop chest" had come from the age of sail, when special scarves and bibs were sold to absorb the tar that dropped from the upper rigging down onto the crew. By law we couldn't increase prices over 10% of what we had ourselves paid for these items. In days of yore captains had overcharged, holding crew members hostage to their pecuniary needs; so politicians a good century ago stepped in to protect the little guy, enacting a law limiting the skippers' profit margins.

After a few weeks Kalbfuss at least looked more appropriate attire-wise, but he never really fit in with either officers or crew on board ship. It didn't take long before all grew tired of his relentless inquiries as to how one felt about virtually everything in life. Within the first month or so he had formulated interesting observations about myself and the crew, and how we related to one another in the chain of command. He had learned the personal backgrounds of some of the mariners, and how they felt about themselves. However, Kalbfuss was really put to the test during typical shipboard disputes, some of them turning violent. Lacking worldly education, he found it unacceptable that one human being could act that way with another. He also seemed miffed that I needed to react aggressively whenever such things occurred on our tanker. The doctor felt it better to talk things out with trouble-makers, figuring there was always some conversational way of diminishing their anger. Of course I'd had much experience of watching macho males beat their chests to show who was bigger, better, and tougher, and knew that only the threat of more power could defuse these tense confrontations at sea. Usually I'd been able to convince hotheads to cool off simply by alluding to a .38 caliber bullet—and Casper knew this.

Over time he distanced himself more and more from us, and began skipping some of his nightly sessions with me. I would then have to order a ship's officer to chase him down and bring him to my cabin. I could see that Kalbfuss was becoming ever more agitated, and less capable of functioning in a milieu like this one. He'd obviously never been in a world of intense labor before, where strict rules and guidelines needed to be followed. The only rules he had had to follow as an adult probably came out of some textbook, and I'm sure those he disagreed with he discarded. Sometimes he seemed to want to reinvent the wheel, asking why certain men worked specific shifts, and why the ship couldn't operate with more flexible work schedules. I could see that Casper's conversations with crew members were confusing him, and I wondered if some of them down below weren't playing with his mind! It got to the point where he suggested that at times certain crewmen should assume the responsibilities of officers, and that it would be a good idea if I occasionally stepped down from my command position, allowing a junior officer to head up the ship for a day. I now believed that despite his credentials, Kalbfuss couldn't quite comprehend the long history of mankind, and how rules of authority make societies at least somewhat functional. His suggestions became so irrationally innovative that I knew he wouldn't survive in an all-male environment, or maybe in *any* real-world environment. I began to consider him disturbed, and things deteriorated so much that I starting acting prankishly myself, reacting to his general thinking and views.

For example, I started removing bullet boxes from the captain's safe, and during my nightly conversations with Casper, would count the bullets. "Let's see," I'd say with a serious look on my face, "is this the same number I had yesterday?" I figured that might help him produce a more exciting report!

Finally I and the chief engineer, a close friend, conspired to send the learned shrink completely round the bend. Whenever he was nearby, we would call each other on the phone, having bizarre conversations. On a couple of occasions I asked the chief engineer if he'd taken the bow of the ship and moved it aft, and when he would complete that job, because I wanted the stern moved forward. After hanging up, I'd look dead serious, telling Kalbfuss, "I don't know what the chief engineer is up to, but he sure isn't doing what I've ordered him to do." The earnest therapist looked terrified! Equally nonsensical ideas were hatched by the chief engineer, and one day Casper informed me that he had been asked to convey a message: that I needed to order more mice! One of the small portable generators had apparently become infected, and the mice left on the generating belt were becoming tired. The chief engineer needed a fresh batch sent out immediately! Relating this message in a serious manner, the doctor seemed to believe every word of it.

About two-thirds into the voyage he became so aberrational that he started skipping meals, maybe feeling that something in the food was creating a problem in crew and officers, which showed up in their verbiage. By this time Kalbfuss probably felt he could survive on munchies I sold from the slop chest, such as potato chips or pretzels. His personal grooming began deteriorating as well. During the voyage he had bought several combs, yet after a month or two at sea his hair was always a mess, and his teeth no longer looked brushed. One day I told him of my legal responsibility to see that the entire ship was in sanitary condition, informing him that even his cabin would come under my scrutiny.

Entering that room, I was dumbfounded to find a total pig sty— combs and toothbrushes everywhere, yet Casper obviously unable to locate a single one! Not to mention empty potato chip bags, or just chips or pretzels in his bunk, and dirty underwear and other clothing piled on the floor. I had to reprimand him for these unsanitary conditions, noting that he would either have to improve, or I'd be obliged to send him home early. When I and the third officer left his room after that inspection, the third officer asked me with concern in his voice: "Is Dr. Kalbfuss OK?" That was a good question, because it was evident he was becoming several bricks short of the proverbial load!

About a week before arrival in our first port of call, after which we would depart again, I wired the home office that we would have to get this Freudian off ship early, several weeks, in fact, before his scheduled itinerary was to end. Kalbfuss was acting strangely, I said, and needed rest time back in familiar surroundings. I suggested that some of his associates meet him at the dock to debrief him, figuring it would require more than one, for he looked extremely confused. How many shrinks *does* it take to straighten out a psychiatrist? I wasn't sure myself.

The last few days Casper was on board things got so bad that we actually had to put him in a straitjacket, which we kept on the ship. Whenever we took him out of his cabin, we put it on him. Sometimes we would then leave it on him all day and only remove it at night. I also ordered my officers to maintain a twenty-four hour watch, for fear that the doctor might jump over the side of the vessel.

Naturally the home office was surprised to hear about Casper's condition, responding that they had notified his psychiatric associates of the problem. Arrangements were made for an ambulance to pull up once the ship docked (in my wire I'd suggested they summon a medical doctor as a precaution, so that the owners might avoid legal responsibilities). Kalbfuss's colleagues indicated they would be there, too.

When the ship docked, there was the ambulance and a knot of people around it. Casper's chief assistant psychiatrist came on board, along with an M.D., and before I allowed the confused shrink to leave the vessel, I had the M.D. and Casper's associate do a preliminary assessment of him in my office. Kalbfuss did not apparently recognize his partner, making me feel that by this time he *had* actually gone bonkers. The doctor checked his blood pressure, breathing, pulse et al., pronouncing him fit enough to depart the ship. However, I insisted that Kalbfuss be placed in a stokeslitter and carried down the ship's gangway, again as a precaution, in case he should fall or trip.

His associate, Dr. Langenbrunner,[17] kept expressing deep concern about Casper's condition, but I couldn't understand why he apologized so repetitively about his broken-down partner. He grew so unctuous that I began feeling uncomfortable. Maybe Langenbrunner had sensed that Kalbfuss was already so unstable that this voyage could do him no good. Or maybe he knew in advance that the man should never have sailed in the first place. Perhaps practicing psychiatrists never stop practising, even on each other. Maybe Langenbrunner himself had sent his partner out to sea as a kind of experiment, leading to the final diagnosis—of full-fledged madness! I wasn't quite sure, but I did get the impression that this associate had helped convince Casper to make the trip.

Before they left, I asked Kalbfuss's partner whether at some point in the future—that is, if they ever got the man completely unwound— he might write an analysis of the situation; if so, I'd like a copy. Failing that, I told Langenbrunner with a chuckle, "There will always be a place for you, too" (on our ship). Very gently he declined the offer, and left with one more apology for his partner's state. During our conversation I had briefly considered spinning the chamber of my pistol, or getting some ball bearings and rolling them in my hands. But I ended up handling the whole situation with as much decorum as I could muster, hoping not to disorient any more psychiatrists!

---

[17]   This is a pseudonym.

Kalbfuss went down in the stokeslitter, and it brought back memories of Captain Crofton carried off with a bullet hole in his head. I'm not sure whether Casper's scrambled brains were in much better shape. And that was the last I saw of this poor doctor.

Later that year, however, I had occasion to discuss the situation with the ship's owner, who informed me that Kalbfuss was still at his place of work, but no longer in a position of authority. Rather, he was now a patient. The owner wanted to know what we had done to him during that voyage to mess up the guy's head so thoroughly. I said something to the effect that "Casper is probably in no worse shape than many of my guys out there. Shoreside people probably don't realize how nutty we all are!"

With a big smile, the genial owner replied, "Oh yes, we do!" And he patted me on the back, telling me: "You're doing a good job, captain." With the wackos, he meant.

In sum, life's storms seem much more unpredictable and intense than real ones. The sun at least rises in the morning in the East, and there are certain scientific predictables that you can ascertain in Mother Nature. But when it comes to human behavior, you can throw all that out the window. This is what my years on the high seas taught me most.

66683921R00107

Made in the USA
Lexington, KY
22 August 2017